Viewpoints U.S.A.
A Basic ESL Reader

Roberta J. Vann

Vivian P. Hefley

Intensive English and Orientation Program
Iowa State University

Viewpoints U.S.A.
A Basic ESL Reader

HEINLE & HEINLE PUBLISHERS
A Division of Wadsworth, Inc.
Boston, Massachusetts 02116

To Maurice Imhoof and Robert Fox,
who opened the door

Sponsoring Editor: Phillip Leininger
Project Editor: Jo-Ann Goldfarb
Designer: Elliot Epstein
Production: Marion A. Palen/Delia Tedoff
Photo Researcher: Mira Schachne
Compositor: ComCom Division of Haddon Craftsmen, Inc.
Printer and Binder: R. R. Donnelley & Sons Company
Art Studio: Fine Line Illustrations, Inc.

Viewpoints U.S.A.: A Basic ESL Reader

Library of Congress Cataloging in Publication Data

Vann, Roberta J., 1947–
  Viewpoints U.S.A.

  1. English language—Text-books for foreign speakers.
2. Readers—United States. 3. United States—Civilization
—Addresses, essays, lectures. I. Hefley, Vivian P.,
1943–   . II. Title. III. Title: Viewpoints USA.
PE1128.V33 1984   428.6′4   83-18531
ISBN 0-8384-3002-3

Photograph Credits
Pages 2–3: Beckwith Studios; *pp. 44–45:* Mellett, Taurus; *p. 74 (top):* Beckwith
Studios; *pp. 74–75* (bottom): UPI; *pp. 90–91:* Forsyth, Monkmeyer; *pp. 106–107:*
© Walt Disney Productions, world rights reserved; *pp. 122–123:* Thom Roberts;
pp. 138–139, 151: courtesy of McDonald's; *p. 156 (top):* © Dietz, Stock, Boston;
p. 156 (bottom): Compagnone, Jeroboam; *pp. 156–157 (top):* © Dietz, Stock,
Boston; *pp. 156–157 (bottom):* © Hankin, Stock, Boston; *p. 184:* Courtesy of
Kaufmann, Lanskey & Baker; *pp. 188–189:* courtesy of Delynn Hefley; *pp.
202–203:* © Spratt, Picture Group; *pp. 216–217:* © Kroll, 1979, Taurus; *pp.
230–231:* courtesy of ISU Photo Service; *pp. 246–247:* Johnson, Leo de Wys Inc.,
pp. 260–261: © Brown, Picture Group.

Contents

To the Instructor

Viewpoints U.S.A. is a reading-skills text for high-beginning and low-intermediate ESL students. Various passages and non-linear texts not only expand the reader's general vocabulary and knowledge of North American life, but also provide practice in skills such as pre-reading, scanning, finding the main idea, and using context clues and affixes to decipher the meanings of new words. The sequential arrangement of *Viewpoints U.S.A.*, with later chapters reviewing and building on the basic vocabulary and simple grammatical structures of the first half of the book, makes it ideal for a two-course sequence.

READING

Certain general assumptions about the reading process of adult second-language learners have shaped this text. First, we assume that adult beginning-ESL students need to view reading not as a mere exercise to improve their English, but as a pleasurable means of acquiring knowledge. Consequently, we have developed material that not only interests mature readers, but controls structure and vocabulary so that students *read* rather than merely decipher. Second, we assume that reading is an active skill involving guessing, predicting, checking, and questioning—skills that many ESL students lack. Thus we have designed exercises following each reading to develop these skills. Third, we assume that ESL readers vary in their individual reading tastes, background, and skill development. Therefore we have created a text that allows for individualization through its wide assortment of exercises.

Topics for the book were inspired by our students' curiosity about certain aspects of North American life ranging from garage sales to rodeos. Common themes unite the two main readings in each of the 18 chapters, with the first reading introducing concepts and vocabulary, and the second reading focusing on a related topic, often written from a different viewpoint. While the major readings consist of passages based on magazine features, students also practice non-linear reading of items such as maps, charts, tables, and ads, using techniques such as scanning, fact finding, and inference making.

EXERCISES

Viewpoints U.S.A. offers a variety of exercises designed to help a wide range of students acquire, practice, and review essential reading skills. We encourage you to individualize instruction by selecting exercises most appropriate to the proficiency level and interests of your students. The most challenging exercises in each chapter are marked with double asterisks (**) to aid you in making selections.

PRE-READING

Goal: To prepare students for what they are about to read and to help them acquire good pre-reading habits, which they can transfer to other kinds of reading.

How: By using pictures, titles, and pre-reading and scanning questions to discover general ideas about the text.

COMPREHENSION

Goal: To address four essential reading skills: overall understanding, fact finding, inference making, and synthesizing background knowledge with information in the passage.

General Questions (Chapters 1–9)

Aim: To check overall understanding.

How: By recognizing ideas from the passage that are true and correcting those that are false.

General Questions (Chapters 10–18)

Aim: To check overall understanding and encourage students to examine the text for a variety of possibly correct responses.

How: By recognizing ideas from the passage that are true and false and expanding those ideas in their own words.

Factual Questions

Aim: To check comprehension of specific facts.

How: By answering factual questions after careful reading or re-reading of the text.

**Inferential Questions

Aim: To develop skill in going beyond words and sentences to understand a passage.

How: By answering inferential questions from knowledge gained from the passage.

Note: Students may read the passage a second time before answering.

What Do You Think?   *Aim:* To synthesize students' prior knowledge of a topic and expand vocabulary and comprehension.

How: By discussing questions in groups either before or after reading the passages.

Main Ideas   *Aim:* To practice separating main ideas from those less important.

How: By re-reading individual paragraphs from the passage and selecting the appropriate choice.

Chapter Review   *Aim:* To provide students with a final opportunity to review a central idea of the main reading.

How: By reconstructing central ideas in their own words.

VOCABULARY SKILLS   *Goal:* To help students expand their vocabulary and acquire strategies for dealing with unfamiliar vocabulary they encounter in reading.

Word Search   *Aim:* To reinforce new vocabulary and scanning techniques while simultaneously providing students with simplified dictionary-like definitions.

How: By scanning to find new vocabulary to match definitions.

Opposites, Word Families, and Affixes   *Aim:* To establish links with related vocabulary items, thus providing memory aids.

How: By matching new vocabulary with their opposites, using related vocabulary, and deciphering the meaning of unknown words by understanding the meaning of their parts.

**Vocabulary in Context   *Aim:* To test students' acquisition of newly learned vocabulary.

How: By using these words in a new context.

Matching Meanings	*Aim:* To help students recognize multiple meanings of vocabulary.
	How: By using context clues in sentences to help determine the appropriate meaning.
Idioms and Expressions	*Aim:* To teach idioms and expressions used in the readings.
	How: By reading explanatory notes, then practicing use in context.
READING SKILLS	*Goal:* To provide practice in using various reading strategies to improve reading proficiency.
Guessing the Meaning from Context	*Aim:* To provide the students with one alternative to dictionary dependence.
	How: By using the context to find clues to the meaning of new vocabulary.
Pronoun Reference, Connections, and Connecting Words	*Aim:* To help students understand cohesive devices in the text.
	How: By discovering pronoun antecedents and other cohesive devices of equivalence.
Scanning	*Aim:* To develop proficiency in scanning.
	How: By practice in looking quickly over a passage to spot specific information, such as a name or a number.
Sentence Splitting	*Aim:* To provide students with a technique for understanding compound and complex sentences.
	How: By breaking compound and complex sentences into more easily understandable syntactic units.
POST-READING ACTIVITIES	*Goal:* To extend opportunities for students to use newly acquired vocabulary and reading skills to new contexts.
Strip Stories, Applications, and Linear Biography	*Aim:* To provide students with extended reading opportunities related to the chapter content.
	How: By filling out forms, completing tables, and solving logic problems.

Puzzles and Games   *Aim:* To provide students with an enjoyable and independent means of reinforcing newly acquired vocabulary.

How: By working puzzles and games and checking answers.

Note: An answer key for the word puzzles and games in the back of this book allows students to work independently on this section.

SAMPLE LESSON PLAN

Day 1   Building a Background

1. (Books closed.) Instructor shows students slides, pictures, or clippings of material relevant to chapter ideas and/or asks questions and elicits discussion concerning general ideas from the reading. Potentially problematic vocabulary can be incorporated into questions and discussion. (Instructors may wish to use some of the "What Do You Think?" or similar questions to elicit discussion.)
2. (Books open.) Instructor initiates the pre-reading exercises with questions about the opening illustration and title. Students scan picture glosses and answer the pre-reading questions.

Reading the Passage

1. Students answer pre-reading scanning questions (not introduced until Chapter 3). To facilitate this process, the instructor may wish to read the questions aloud while the students locate the answers.
2. Instructor reminds students to think about initial questions while reading the passage.
3. Students read the passage silently.
4. Instructor explains or demonstrates any problematic vocabulary. (A bilingual dictionary should be used only as a last resort.)
5. Instructor may wish to read the passage aloud as students follow along in their books.
6. Instructor repeats initial questions for students to answer.

Checking Comprehension

1. Students answer general questions either orally or on paper.
2. Instructor may wish to have students re-read the passage silently before answering the remainder of the questions.
3. Students answer Inferential Questions if their language proficiency permits.

4. Students and teachers explore cross-cultural differences with "What Do You Think?" discussion questions.

Day 2 **Expanding Vocabulary and Reading Skills**

Students do vocabulary and reading skills exercises orally or in writing.

Day 3 **Reading the Second Passage**

Instructor may follow the same steps as for reading the first passage or may make adjustments depending on class needs.

Expanding Vocabulary and Reading Skills

Students do exercises orally or in writing, in class or for homework.

Day 4 **Completing the Chapter**

1. Students complete any remaining skills exercises.
2. Students do the Chapter Review—orally or in writing, in class or for homework.
3. Students do assigned post-reading activities. (Games and Puzzles are done individually.)

Note: An instructor's manual, providing an answer key and suggestions for using exercises, accompanies *Viewpoints U.S.A.* Copies may be obtained from Harper & Row.

Acknowledgments

We wish to thank the many people who have contributed to *Viewpoints U.S.A.* Their insights and encouragement have been invaluable.

We extend our sincere thanks to Iowa State University and our colleagues in the Department of English and in the Intensive English and Orientation Program, who commented on earlier drafts or class-tested materials for us. Included are: Mary Barratt, Wesley Freemeyer, Marge Graves, Chris Martin, Barbara Matthies, and Julia Waggoner. Thanks also to Marilyn Dale for her help in typing. Daisy Meyer deserves special thanks for her many hours of effort and dedication and for her valuable insights.

We also thank the following people: Ralph P. Barrett, Michigan State University; Linda Lonon Blanton, University of New Orleans; John G. Bordie, the University of Texas at Austin; Charles Haynes, American Language Institute, New York University; John Homan, Florida International University, Tamiani Campus; William W. Jex, American Language Institute, New York University; Bertha C. Neustadt, Boston University; Thomas Scovel, San Francisco State University; and Julie Weismann, Triton College—all these colleagues in English as a second language gave generously of their time and influenced *Viewpoints U.S.A.* through their critiques of earlier drafts.

Finally, we wish to thank the editorial staff of Harper & Row for encouragement and support.

Roberta J. Vann
Vivian P. Hefley

Viewpoints U.S.A.
A Basic ESL Reader

Books for a Dime, *modest* Clothes for a Dollar

PRE-READING

In the picture there are many items for sale.
Give the prices of these items:

bathtub	_____	lawnmower	_____
dress	_____	plant	_____
hat	_____	small table	_____
lamp	_____	suitcase	_____

Where can you buy books for a dime or clothes for a dollar?

3

READING 1

Read the passage carefully to learn the answer to this question:

Why do some people have garage sales?

[1] Sometimes people need a special item for their house, apartment, or office. They may need some dishes or a small table for the living room. They may need some clothes for the children or a small rug for the office. People can buy these items new at a store, but they are usually expensive. Some people do not have the money to buy these things new, and some people do not want to spend a lot of money. These people go to a garage or yard sale.

[2] A garage or yard sale is a good place to buy inexpensive, used items. People can buy pots and pans° for the kitchen or plants for the living room. They can buy almost anything: furniture, cassettes, radios, sinks, or old magazines.

Pot and pan

[3] Where do people find the items to sell? Often people find these items in their closets or drawers, and in their basements or garages. They usually find a lot of old, useless items. They collect all these things and look at them carefully. They may keep some of the things and sell the others at a garage sale.

[4] Some people do not like to throw old things away, so they sell them at a garage sale. "Aha!" somebody says. "Here's an old picture of Aunt Lucy. We don't need this useless picture, so let's sell it. Maybe somebody wants to buy it."

[5] Most of the items at a garage sale are useful, but some of them are useless. Most people at garage sales buy only necessary and useful items. Some people like to collect old things, and some people go only to look.

COMPREHENSION CHECK

General Questions Mark these statements TRUE or FALSE. Correct the false statements. Don't look back at the passage. Follow these examples:

> STATEMENT: People can buy items new at a store.
>
> STUDENT: *True.* (People can buy items new at a store.)
>
> STATEMENT: Items at a store are usually inexpensive.
>
> STUDENT: *False.* Items at a store are usually expensive.

1. _____ A garage sale is a good place to find new items.

2. _____ People can buy almost anything at a garage sale.

3. _____ People find old items in their houses.

4. _____ Some people have garage sales because they don't like to throw old things away.

5. _____ Some people go to garage sales only to look.

Factual Questions Answer these questions. You may look back at the passage.

1. What can people buy at a garage sale?
2. Where do people find the items to sell?
3. What do some people do with all their old things?
4. What do most people buy at garage sales?
5. What do some people like to collect?

** Inferential Questions* Answer these questions. Read the passage again if necessary.

1. Why do people go to garage sales?
2. Why do people usually have a lot of useless items in their houses?
3. Why do some people buy old pictures, old dishes, or old books?

What Do You Think? 1. Do people in your country have garage sales?
2. What do people in your country do with all their old things?

*Note: Double asterisks (**) indicate a more challenging exercise.

VOCABULARY SKILLS   Use the reading passage on page 4 to find these words.

Word Search   1. Write the word in line 8 that means the same as *cheap*.

   _____

2. Write the words in line 9 that mean *items used for cooking*.

   _____

3. Write the words in line 13 that are *places to keep things*.

   _____

4. Write the word in line 23 that means the same as *bring together*.

   _____

Idioms and Expressions   to have a _____; having a _____

   Examples

   1. Some people *have a* garage sale.
   2. My friends *are having a* garage sale this afternoon.

We use this expression with special social activities:

party	birthday party
dance	meeting
picnic	barbecue

Use the listed words in the following conversation:

MARY: We're having a _____ Saturday. Can you come?

JOHN: Yes, I can.
   or
   I'm sorry. I'm busy.

Opposites   Fill in the blanks with the appropriate word:

(expensive/inexpensive)   1. Here are two coats. The

_____ coat costs $5.00. The

other coat costs $50.00.

(keep/throw away)   2. These shoes are old, but they are comfortable. I like them very much. I want

to _____ them.

(useful/useless)   3. My pen is out of ink. It's

_____.

(buy/sell)   4. Let's find a garage sale. I want to

_____ a lamp for the living

room.

(new/used)   5. I don't have much money. I can't buy

a _____ TV.

Matching Meanings   Sometimes English words can have more than one meaning. Follow this example:

A. a month   B. have a possibility to

<u>A</u>   *May* has 31 days.

<u>B</u>   Some people *may* need some clothes for their children.

<u>B</u>   John *may* buy this book about balloons.

Match the meaning with each sentence:

A. space   B. part of a building

___ 1. This house has five *rooms.*

___ 2. There's no *room* for this chair.

___ 3. Do you have *room* for another person?

      A. see   B. appear

__ 4. John *looks* at all the items for sale.

__ 5. These spoons *look* old.

__ 6. That old woman *looks* poor.

      A. type, sort   B. good

__ 7. What *kind* of suit do you want?

__ 8. My father is a *kind* man.

__ 9. There are different *kinds* of books in the box.

      A. without money   B. bad

__ 10. The food at that restaurant is very *poor*.

__ 11. The old woman is *poor*.

__ 12. This is a *poor* table. It's broken.

READING SKILLS

Pronoun Reference   Follow this example:

> People can buy these items at a store, but (they) are usually
> expensive.

People sometimes need a special item for (their) house, apartment, or office. (They) can buy (it) at a store or at a garage sale.

Most people find items to sell in (their) houses. (They) collect all the items and look at (them) carefully.

My neighbor has an old picture. (She) doesn't want to keep (it), so (she) is going to sell (it) at her next garage sale.

Main Ideas Choose the main idea. The main idea of

1. paragraph 1 is:
   a. People can buy items new at a store.
   b. People need some dishes.
   c. People go to garage sales to buy things they need.

2. paragraph 3 is:
   a. People sell items.
   b. People find items for garage sales in their houses.
   c. People find things in their basements.

3. paragraph 5 is:
   a. People go to garage sales for different reasons.
   b. People find items at garage sales.
   c. Some people go to garage sales only to look.

Scanning Look at these questions. Quickly find the answers in the paragraph. Circle the answers when you find them. DON'T READ every word. Follow this example:

When does the garage sale begin?

A.M. = before noon
P.M. = after noon

My friends usually begin their garage sale at 8 A.M., but a lot of people come earlier. Sometimes my friends have some good things for sale, so many people come before 8 o'clock to look at them.

How many suits are there?

There are some clothes over there. I see 3 suits, some dresses, and a lot of children's clothes. A woman is looking at the children's clothes. Her children are looking at the clothes, too.

How much is the toaster?

On this table are some items for the kitchen. Here are some dishes and some pots and pans. Over there is a coffee pot and a toaster. The

$ = dollar

price of the toaster is $3.00. That's cheap for a toaster.

How much does the book about balloons cost?

Here's a box of books under the table. Books are always interesting to look at. There are children's books, schoolbooks, and other kinds of books. Hmmm! Here's an interesting book about balloons. It's only 25¢. I'm going to buy it.

¢ = cent

READING 2

Read this passage carefully to learn the answer to this question:

Why is the neighbor surprised?

My Neighbor's Garage Sale

My neighbor across the street is having a garage sale. Let's go   1
there and look at all the items for sale.

There are a lot of things for sale today. There are some clothes
over there. There are some dresses, shoes, hats, and sweaters. Under
that table is a box of books. There are a lot of books. Here is an   5
interesting book about photography.

Look at this! Here is a picture of Aunt Lucy. Who wants to buy this
old thing? Maybe someone likes to collect old pictures.

On this table there are some items for the kitchen. There are some
dishes, some cups, four old spoons, and a coffee pot.   10

Look at the old woman near the coffee pot. Her dress is very old,
and her sweater has holes.° She wants to buy the coffee pot, but she
does not have much money. The coffee pot costs $4.00, but my friend
sells it to her for only $1.50.

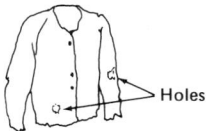

Now the old woman is walking away. Look! She is getting into that   15
big, expensive car. Look at my neighbor's face. He is very surprised.

Garage sales are interesting, but sometimes the people at garage
sales are more interesting.

Holes

COMPREHENSION CHECK

Answer these questions. You may look back at the passage.

1. Who is having a garage sale?
2. Where does he live?
3. Where are the books?
4. How much does the coffee pot cost?
5. How much does the old woman pay for the coffee pot?
6. Is the old woman poor? How do you know?

VOCABULARY SKILLS

Money

=   equals

Example

A half-dollar equals fifty cents. (___50___¢)

Fill in the blanks with the appropriate number:

1. A dime equals ten cents. (_____¢)

2. A penny equals one cent. (_____¢)

3. A quarter equals twenty-five cents. (_____¢)

4. A nickel equals five cents. (_____¢)

5. A dime is the same as _____ cents.

6. There are _____ quarters in a dollar.

7. A nickel and a dime equal _____ cents.

8. A quarter pays for a _____-cent candy bar.

9. Two half-dollars, 5 quarters, 6 dimes, and 3 nickels equal _____ dollars.

READING SKILLS

Prices

Examples

$4.00 = four dollars
$4.75 = four dollars and seventy-five cents

Read these prices out loud:

$1.00	$3.49	$7.17
$6.95	$5.95	$2.39
$0.38	$4.48	$39.95
$1.99	$0.88	$1.08

CHAPTER REVIEW

1. List items you might find at a garage sale:

   _____

   _____

   _____

   _____

   _____

2. List reasons people go to garage sales:

   _____

   _____

   _____

   _____

   _____

POST-READING ACTIVITIES

Word Game   The words on the right each contain AN. Read the clues and complete the words on the right. Follow this example:

something sweet to eat   C A N D Y

1. Mary _____ John   A N __

2. something you cook with   __ A N

3. something with five fingers   __ A N __

4. something green for the garden   __ __ A N __

5. need   __ A N __

6. not dirty   __ __ __ A N

7. something you say after a question   A N __ __ __ __

8. a lot   __ A N __

Crossword Puzzle   Fill in the blanks with the correct words. Find the hidden word.

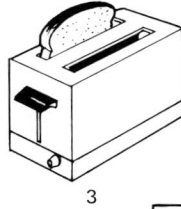

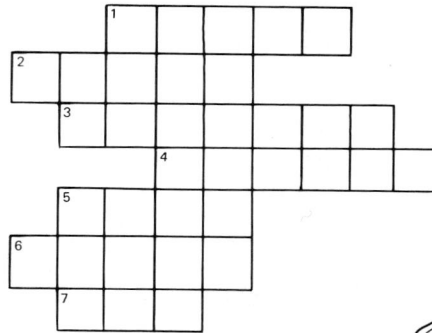

Hidden word

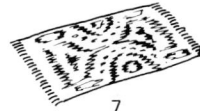

CAMP TELLACOMP

Boys & Girls — Ages 9–17

1

Summer of Fun
and Learning

ON SPRING LAKE
Early Reservations Recommended

A Summer of Fun and Learning

PRE-READING

Look at this ad for a camp. Write the number of the activity next to
  each picture.

1. boating	6. hockey	11. soccer
2. computer science	7. reading	12. tennis
3. flying	8. riding	13. basketball
4. golf	9. riflery	14. water skiing
5. gymnastics	10. scuba diving	15. wrestling

Where can boys and girls have a summer of fun?
What sports activities can they participate in?
What other activities can they participate in?

READING 1   Read the passage carefully to learn the answer to this question:

What do children do during the summer?

Ghost

Handicapped

¹ It is summer vacation and schools are closed. During the summer some children stay home, watch TV, and play with their friends. Some participate in a neighborhood sports program, and some go to camp.

² A camp is a summer vacation place for children. Campers participate in sports activities like swimming, boating, or riding horses. They also take part in other activities like playing games and painting pictures. In the evening they sit around a campfire, cook hot dogs, sing songs, or tell ghost° stories.

³ Some camps combine special programs with the usual camp activities. There are camps to teach tennis, basketball, or other sports. There are camps to teach science or music. There are also camps for intelligent children, fat children, or handicapped° children.

⁴ Now there are computer camps. Denison Bollay owns a computer camp. At his camp children learn how to use computers. Computers are very important today, so children must learn how to use them. Many schools have computers for the students to use, but not all the students know how to use them. Some schools do not have a program to teach the students. So, Bollay's camp combines important computer learning with summer fun.

⁵ Bollay's campers have three computer classes a day. They study computer language and programming. After a few days of classes, each camper designs a computer program. Some campers design programs to help parents at home. Others design programs to help students at school. Some campers design computer games.

⁶ Bollay's campers must also choose two camp activities a day. They can choose an activity like swimming, boating, painting, or horseback riding. In their free time, the campers can choose any activity. What do they do in their free time? Well, they do not swim, and they do not ride horses. They play games on the computers.

**COMPREHENSION
CHECK**

General Questions   Mark these statements TRUE or FALSE. Correct the false statements. Don't look back at the passage. Follow these examples:

STATEMENT: Volleyball is a sports activity.

STUDENT: *True.* (Volleyball is a sports activity.)

STATEMENT: Schools are open during the summer.

STUDENT: *False.* Schools are closed during the summer.

1. _____ Children go to school during the summer.

2. _____ Some camps have special programs.

3. _____ Denison Bollay owns a camp.

4. _____ Computers aren't important today.

5. _____ Campers can choose different activities.

Factual Questions   Answer these questions. You may look back at the passage.

1. What is a camp?
2. What do campers do in the evening?
3. What special programs do some camps have?
4. What two things does Bollay's camp combine?
5. How many classes a day do the campers have?
6. What does each camper do after a few days of classes?
7. What activities can Bollay's campers choose?

∗∗ Inferential Questions   Answer these questions. Read the passage again if necessary.

1. What do campers do during the day?
2. Why does Bollay's camp teach children how to use computers?
3. Why do Bollay's campers play computer games in their free time?

What Do You Think?   1. Are there summer camps in your country? What activities do the
camps have? Do some camps have special programs?
2. Watching TV is an example of an indoor activity. What indoor
activity do you like? What outdoor activity do you like?
3. Do you know how to use a computer? Is it important for students
or children to learn how to use them? Why or why not?

VOCABULARY SKILLS

Word Search

1. Write the word in line 1 that means *not open.*

   _____

2. Write the word in line 3 that means *an area where people live together.*

   _____

3. Write the word in line 10 that means *join together.*

   _____

4. Write the words in line 23 that mean *two or three.*

   _____

5. Write the word in line 24 that means *make.*

   _____

6. Write the word in line 27 that means *have to.*

   _____

7. Write the word in line 27 that means *pick.*

   _____

Idioms and Expressions *free time* = time *not* for sleeping, eating, working, or studying

Examples

1. Most people have some *free time* in the evening.
2. Some people read in their *free time.*
3. Some people watch TV in their *free time.*

Answer these questions.

1. What do campers do in their free time?
2. What do you do in your free time in the evening? On Saturday or Sunday?
3. When do you have the most free time?

** Verbs → Nouns   You can change many verbs to nouns by adding *-ing*.

swim (verb)   Chris likes to *swim*.
swimming (noun)   Chris likes *swimming*.

Fill in the blanks with the appropriate word:

(learn/learning)   1. At some camps you can _____ how to ride horses.

(ride/riding)   2. One of Chris's favorite activities is horseback _____.

(fish/fishing)   3. _____ is a popular sport for many people.

(write/writing)   4. Most campers must _____ letters to their parents once a week.

(play/playing)   5. Children like to _____ all kinds of games.

(learn/learning)   6. Camp Einstein campers _____ different computer languages.

(play/playing)   7. Do you like _____ games such as Monopoly?

(ride/riding)   8. Elephant _____ is not popular in the United States.

(write/writing)   9. Please _____ your name at the top of the page.

(smoke/smoking)   10. No _____

READING SKILLS

Pronoun Reference   Follow this example:

In (their) free time the campers choose any activity (they) want.

Denison Bollay owns a computer camp. At (his) camp children learn how to use computers. Computers are important today, so children must know how to use (them). Many schools have computers for the students to use, but (they) do not know how to use (them).

Connecting Words   Use *and* to connect words or ideas together.

Examples

There are old ladies *and* young children.
          word   +   word

He likes swimming *and* he swims every day.
          idea   +   idea

Match the ideas in column A with the ideas in column B.

Column A	*Column B*
f 1. Some children stay home, and	a. other campers design games.
___ 2. Some campers design programs, and	b. throw away the useless ones.
___ 3. Some people buy things, and	c. ride horses.
___ 4. People keep useful items and	d. tell ghost stories.
___ 5. At night campers sing songs and	e. some people sell things.
___ 6. In their free time, campers can swim and	f. some go to camp.

Main Ideas   Choose the main idea. The main idea of

1. paragraph 1 is:
   a. It's summer vacation.
   b. There are many summer activities for children.
   c. Some children participate in a neighborhood sports program.

2. paragraph 3 is:
   a. Some camps have special programs.
   b. Children like camp.
   c. There are camps for handicapped children.

3. paragraph 5 is:
   a. Computers are important.
   b. The campers study a computer language.
   c. Campers have to design a computer program.

4. paragraph 6 is:
   a. Camps have many activities.
   b. Campers must choose two activities each day.
   c. Campers must choose two sports activities.

Scanning   Look at the following questions. Quickly find the answers in the paragraphs. Circle the answers when you find them. Don't read every word.

Who is going to camp?

How long is he going to be at camp?

It is June 20th, and Chris is going to camp. He cannot eat his breakfast because he is very excited. Chris and his parents are going to leave at 8:00 A.M. The camp is only 200 miles (321.8 km) from their house, so they are going by car. Chris is going to be at the camp for 2 weeks.

How many campers are eating lunch?

How many roommates does Chris have?

It is 12 o'clock, and all 80 campers are eating lunch in the big dining room. Four campers are sitting at each table. Chris is sitting at the table with his 3 roommates. Everyone is talking a lot. There is a lot of noise in the dining room.

What time is it?

Who is Chris's teacher?

Now it is 1 o'clock, and lunch is finished. All the campers are going to their first class. Some campers know how to use a computer. They are in Mr. Buck's class. Chris and the other campers are learning how to use computers. They are in Mrs. Donaldson's class.

READING 2

Read this letter to learn the answer to this question:

Where is Chris?

Dear Mom and Dad,   1

It's after lunch. Everyone is writing letters in the dining room. We have to write home every week, so here's my first letter.

I have three roommates. Two of them know how to use comput-ers. They are in Mr. Buck's class. I'm studying BASIC. That's a com-   5 puter language.

I have to design my own program this week. All of the campers have to. I want to design a game. Then I can teach it to you.

We have to pick two other activities every day. I usually pick swimming, boating, horseback riding, or baseball. In my free time,   10 I play games on the computers. Most of the campers do.

I like camp, but I don't like the food. It's terrible!

I have to say "good-bye" now. Everybody's going outside. See you in two weeks.

Love,   15

Chris

P.S. = something you for-got to say in your letter

P.S. Don't forget to send my new tennis shoes.

COMPREHENSION CHECK

Answer these questions. You may look back at the passage.

1. What does Chris have to do every week?
2. How many roommates does Chris have?
3. What is BASIC?
4. What kind of program does Chris want to design?
5. Which activities does Chris usually pick?
6. What does Chris think about the food?
7. What do most of the campers do in their free time?
8. When does camp end?

VOCABULARY SKILLS

Matching Meanings   These italicized words have more than one meaning. Match the correct meaning with each sentence.

A. look at   B. something to show time

___ 1. The camper took off his *watch*.

___ 2. The boys like to *watch* TV in their free time.

___ 3. Is that a new *watch*?

A. metal container   B. know how to

___ 4. I need a *can* of tomatoes.

___ 5. *Can* you swim?

___ 6. Chris *can* play games on the computer.

A. not busy   B. without cost

___ 7. The campers have a lot of *free* time.

___ 8. The books in this box are *free*.

___ 9. When are you *free*?

A. course   B. one kind of plant or animal

___ 10. All birds are in the same *class*.

___ 11. What *class* are you taking?

___ 12. Mary is in English *class* right now.

A. free space   B. particular spot or area

___ 13. I can't find a *place* to put these books.

___ 14. Camp is a *place* for children.

___ 15. I know a good *place* to eat.

Numbers   What number does each word equal?

pair	_2_	quarter	___
dime	___	twice	___

noon _____   single _____

cent _____   nickel _____

once _____   half-dollar _____

READING SKILLS

Reduced Sentences   Look at these examples:

I'm going to camp, but my sister isn't.

Where isn't my sister going? *to camp* _____

In my free time, I play games on the computers. Most of the campers do.

What do most of the campers do? *play games* _____

Read each sentence or sentences and answer the questions:

1. I have to design a program. All the campers have to.
   What do all the campers have to do?

   _____

2. Everyone is going outside and Chris is, too.
   Where is Chris going?

   _____

3. Let's buy this cheap toaster. Oh, we can't.
   What can't we buy?

   _____

4. Some campers know how to use a computer, but Chris doesn't.
   What doesn't Chris know how to do?

   _____

5. Chris isn't designing a program to help his mother, but his roommate is.
   What is his roommate doing?

   _____

6. Chris can choose any activity, and the other campers can, too.
   What can the other campers choose?

   _____

Scanning

```
CAMP TELLACOMP

BOYS & GIRLS 8–15
A SUMMER OF CAMP FUN
LOCATED ON 50 ACRES NEAR SPRING
LAKE IN BLUE ROCK
1–3 WEEK SESSIONS 1 WK/$195,
2 WKS/$353, 3 WKS/$505.
HORSES, SWIMMING, WATER SKIING,
BACKPACKING, BOATING, FISHING,
ARTS & CRAFTS.

CALL OR WRITE FOR BROCHURE:
CAMP TELLACOMP
P.O. BOX 5152      (719) 324-7283
```

Here is an ad for a camp. Scan the ad to answer these questions:

1. Can a girl 12 years old go to the camp?
2. Is the camp near Blue Rock Lake?
3. How much does it cost to go to camp for 2 weeks?
4. What activities are water activities?
5. You want to paint a picture. What activity would you choose?
6. What number do you call for more information about the camp? What does the camp send?
7. What are the abbreviations for these words?

   week = _____

   post office = _____

8. What does the symbol "&" mean?
9. Which is cheaper: three 1-week sessions or one 3-week session?

CHAPTER REVIEW

1. Tell something about camps.

   _____

   _____

2. List some camp activities:

   _____

   _____

   _____

   _____

3. Tell something about Denison Bollay's camp.

   _____

   _____

POST-READING ACTIVITIES

You want more information about Camp Tellacomp. Fill out this postcard:

Please send me a free brochure about your camp.

NAME _____

ADDRESS _____

CITY _____

STATE _____ ZIP _____

Stamp

CAMP TELLACOMP
P.O. Box 5152
Katchwa, Illinois
                32759

Computer Game   Bollay's campers like to play tricks such as this one on their computers. You can try this same trick on a calculator.

Directions	*Example*
1. Enter any 3-digit number on the calculator.	789
2. Enter it again so it becomes a 6-digit number.	789789
3. Divide that number by 7.	$\div\ 7 = 112827$
4. Divide the new number by 11.	$\div\ 11 = 10257$
5. Divide the new number by the original number.	$\div\ 789 = 13$
6. The answer will be 13.	

You can try this same trick with any 3 numbers, and the answer will always be 13.

Word Search Puzzle Read the list of words on the left. Look for these words in the block of letters on the right. Circle the words you find. The words can go forward, or backward, or up, or down. Follow the example.

computer | E | T | A | P | I | C | I | T | R | A | P
summer | X | T | C | I | V | H | S | E | M | A | G
camp | K | B | T | U | C | I | L | M | E | S | R
children | V | I | I | L | O | L | E | A | R | N | P
activities | A | D | V | K | M | D | O | T | L | E | S
~~learn~~ | C | Y | I | J | P | R | F | F | C | O | U
fun | A | C | T | O | U | E | S | C | A | F | M
program | T | C | I | O | T | N | U | F | M | O | M
games | I | L | E | F | E | K | I | N | P | I | E
special | O | M | S | P | R | O | G | R | A | M | R
vacation | N | F | S | P | E | C | I | A | L | V | Z
participate | | | | | | | | | | |

Strawberries: Pick Them Yourself!

bài, cây dâu tây

PRE-READING

Label the picture on the left with the correct word below.

basket   strawberries   face
rows of plants   arm   hand

Where are the women?
What are they doing?

31

READING 1

Scan the passage to find the answers to these questions:

1. Who owns the farm?
2. How many acres of strawberries does the owner have?

Now, read the passage carefully to learn the answers to these questions:

1. Why do people pick strawberries?
2. What kind of people pick strawberries?

Crawling between rows

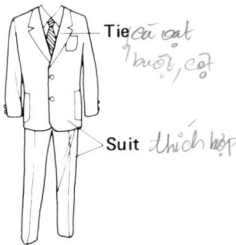

Tie

Suit

¹ It is a beautiful day in June. The sun is hot. The strawberries are   1
ripe, and the strawberry fields are full of people. These people are
picking strawberries. They are not farmers or farm workers, and they
are not picking the fruit for money. They are picking fruit for fun.
They can buy strawberries in a supermarket, but it is cheaper to pick   5
their own fruit. Strawberries from the farm are also fresher. Most
people also like to pick their own fruit because it is a pleasant way
to spend an afternoon.

² One little boy is crawling° between the rows of plants. He is
picking the berries and eating them as fast as he can. Two young   10
women in pretty dresses and high-heeled shoes are getting out of
their car. Now they are taking off their shoes. These women are
taking a break from their work. They want to pick fruit and enjoy the
sunshine.

³ Every day during the strawberry season, cars wait next to a big   15
building on the farm. The building has three giant strawberries on
it. The people in the cars are waiting. They want a place to park and
a chance to pick strawberries.

⁴ Bob Furleigh is the owner of the strawberry farm. Mr. Furleigh
says many different kinds of people stop to pick his strawberries.   20
There are grandmothers in big straw hats and young children in
jeans. They enjoy spending the day outdoors. Sometimes there are
businessmen in suits° and ties.° They stop to pick strawberries on their
way home from work.

⁵ Mr. Furleigh has 28 acres (11.34 ha) of strawberries. Last year he   25
sold 12,000 pounds (5443.11 kg) of fruit in one day and 10,000 pounds
(4535.92 kg) the next day. One couple picked 145 pounds (65.77 kg)
by themselves.

⁶ "It really makes me feel good to see all these happy people out
here," says Mr. Furleigh.   30

Adapted from the *Des Moines Register*

COMPREHENSION CHECK

General Questions Mark these statements TRUE or FALSE. Correct the false statements. Don't look back at the passage.

1. _F_ The people are picking strawberries to earn money.
2. _T_ A little boy is in the strawberry field.
3. _F_ Only grandmothers are picking strawberries.
4. _T_ People in cars want a chance to pick strawberries.
5. _T_ The building on the Furleigh farm has three big strawberries on it.
6. _T_ A man owns the strawberry farm.
7. _T_ Businessmen stop to pick strawberries.
8. _F_ Last year Mr. Furleigh did not sell much fruit.
9. _T_ Mr. Furleigh likes to see happy people on his farm.

Factual Questions Answer these questions. You may look back at the passage.

1. What are the people doing in the strawberry fields?
2. Where can you get the freshest fruit?
3. What is the little boy doing?
4. What are the two young women wearing?
5. Where do the cars wait?
6. When do businessmen often stop to pick strawberries?

** Inferential Questions Answer these questions. Read the passage again if necessary.

1. What kind of day is it?
2. What were the two young women doing before coming to pick strawberries?
3. Why is Mr. Furleigh happy?

What Do You Think?
1. Are strawberries popular in your home country? Why or why not? What is the most popular fruit?
2. Do people in your home country sometimes pick fruit or vegetables for recreation?

3. In your home country:
   Do businessmen ever pick fruit?
   Do city people ever go to the country to pick fruit?
   Do children or older people ever pick fruit?
4. Is picking fruit a pleasant way to spend an afternoon for you?
5. Will picking fruit for fun be more popular in a technological or an agricultural society? Why?

VOCABULARY SKILLS

Word Search

1. Write the word in line 5 that means *grocery store*.

   Supermarket

2. Write the word in line 9 that means *moving on hands and feet* as babies do before they learn to walk.

   _____

3. Write the word in line 9 that means *a group of things in a line*.

   _____

4. Write the word in line 14 that means *bright light from the sun*.

   _____

5. Write the word in line 16 that means *very big*.

   _____

6. Write the word in line 25 that means *a unit of land about 4000 square meters*.

   _____

7. Write the word in line 26 that means *almost $\frac{1}{2}$ kilogram*.

   _____

Opposites   We make the opposites of many English words by adding the prefix *un-*:

>   necessary → unnecessary

Follow this example:

(necessary/unnecessary)   For some students, a car may be useful, but a Rolls Royce is probably *unnecessary*.

Fill in the blanks with the appropriate word:

(important/unimportant)   1. Joe plays tennis indoors, so for him the weather does not matter. The most ＿＿＿＿＿＿ thing for him is to win the game.

(usual/unusual)   2. Cats or dogs are typical pets in the United States. Tigers and elephants are ＿＿＿＿＿＿ pets.

(pleasant/unpleasant)   3. I like nice weather for picnics. In ＿＿＿＿＿＿ weather, I prefer to stay home in bed.

(interesting/uninteresting)   4. Boring films put me to sleep, but I do like ＿＿＿＿＿＿ ones.

(intelligent/unintelligent)   5. Rabbits seem to be stupid animals, but monkeys are ＿＿＿＿＿＿.

(happy/unhappy)   6. I am a farmer. I like lots of sunshine and rain, but too much sunshine or rain makes me ＿＿＿＿＿＿.

∗∗ Vocabulary in	take a break	ripe	supermarket	farmers
Context	take off	row	pick	

Fill in the blanks with the appropriate word:

1. We are tomato _____. First, we plant our young

   tomatoes. Each _____ of tomato plants must be straight.

   Next, we water the young plants and wait about two months.

   When the tomatoes are red, they are _____, and we

   _____ them. Finally, we sell them to a large

   _____. This is the way we make our money.

2. John studies too much. I told him to _____. I told him to

   go home, _____ his shoes, have a cup of tea, and relax.

Matching Meanings   These italicized words have more than one meaning. Match the
correct meaning with each sentence.

   A. fourths   B. 25-cent pieces

   __ 1. Tom has four *quarters* in his pocket.

   __ 2. Jack is cutting paper into *quarters*.

   __ 3. I am hungry. I can eat three-*quarters* of that cake.

   A. choose   B. harvest

   __ 4. Mary likes to *pick* her own clothes.

   __ 5. Farmers *pick* strawberries early in the morning.

   __ 6. Are you going to *pick* apples? Don't forget to take a basket
   with you.

A. public garden   B. put

B 7. We can *park* the car over there.

A 8. The children played in the *park*.

A 9. People are having picnics in the *park*.

A. remove   B. go up into the air

A 10. *Take off* your shoes and relax.

B 11. The plane *takes off* at 7 o'clock.

A 12. The children go into the house and *take off* their coats.

A. two   B. husband and wife

B 13. One *couple* picked 145 pounds by themselves.

A 14. I want a *couple* of strawberries.

___15. They are a happy *couple*.

READING SKILLS

Pronoun Reference Follow this example:

These people are picking strawberries. But they are not picking strawberries to earn money.

One little boy is crawling between the rows of plants. He is picking the berries and eating them as fast as he can. Two young women in pretty dresses and high-heeled shoes are getting out of their car and taking off their shoes. These women are taking a break from their work. They want to pick fruit and enjoy the sunshine.

Connecting Words   Look at this sentence:

> Most of the items in the garage are useful, *but* some are not.

We use the word *but* to connect sentences together. The second sentence is usually an opposite idea.

Match the ideas in Column A with the opposite idea in Column B.

	Column A	*Column B*
d 1.	You can buy strawberries in a supermarket, but	a. the students don't know how to use them.
___ 2.	The coffee pot costs $4.75, but	b. there isn't any.
___ 3.	Many schools have computers, but	c. my neighbors are selling it for $2.00.
___ 4.	The old woman looks poor, but	d. it is cheaper to pick your own.
___ 5.	These words have the same pronunciation, but	e. she drives an expensive car.
___ 6.	I'd like a cup of coffee, but	f. they have a different spelling.

Main Ideas   Choose the main idea. The main idea of

1. paragraph 1 is:
   a. People pick strawberries for different reasons.
   b. It is a beautiful day in June.
   c. The strawberries are ripe.

2. paragraph 4 is:
   a. Mr. Furleigh owns the strawberry farm.
   b. Young children enjoy spending the day outdoors.
   c. Many different kinds of people stop to pick Mr. Furleigh's strawberries.

3. the whole passage is:
   a. Last year people picked 145 pounds of strawberries by themselves.
   b. Lots of people enjoy picking their own strawberries.
   c. Picking your own strawberries saves lots of money.

READING 2 Read this recipe quickly to learn how to make strawberry shortcake:

Strawberry Shortcake (6 Servings)

1 plain cake
1 quart (946 ml) strawberries
$\frac{1}{2}$ cup (118 ml) sugar
$1\frac{3}{4}$ cups (414 ml) cream

1. Cut up the strawberries.
2. Mix the strawberries with $\frac{1}{2}$ cup sugar.
3. Cut the cake in half.
4. Beat the cream until it is thick.
5. Put half of the cake on a large plate.
6. Put half of the strawberries on the cake.
7. Put half of the cream on top.
8. Put the other half of the cake on top of the cream.
9. Repeat steps 6 and 7.
10. Put a few whole strawberries on top.

COMPREHENSION CHECK Answer these questions. Look back at the recipe if necessary.

1. How many servings will this recipe make?
2. How many ingredients are in this recipe?
3. How many of these ingredients are liquid?
4. What is the first thing you do with the strawberries?
5. What do you do with the cream?
6. What do you do in step 9?

VOCABULARY SKILLS

Numbers Write the word for each number:

1 - _____   1st - _____

2 - _____   2nd - _____

3 - _____   3rd - _____

4 - _____   4th - _____

5 - *five*   5th - *fifth*

6 - *six*	6th - _____
7 - _____	7th - _____
8 - _____	8th- _____
9 - _____	9th - *ninth*
10 - _____	10th - _____

Write the correct form of the number in parentheses.
Follow this example:

There are (7) ___*seven*___ students in the class. Jose is the (7) ___*seventh*___ student.

Joe is (9) _____ years old and in the (4) _____ grade at school. There are (10) _____ boys in his class. Joe sits in the (3) _____ row of the class at the (2) _____ desk. (4) _____ boys sit behind him. Joe has (5) _____ classes at school. He is good in all (5) _____ subjects, but his favorite one is math. He has math during the (3) _____ hour, right before lunch.

Complete this recipe. Start with the word *first*. Use other numbers like *second*, *third*, etc., and words like *then*, *next*, and *finally*.

This is how to make strawberry shortcake. _____, cut up one quart of strawberries. _____, mix them with $\frac{1}{2}$ cup of sugar. _____, cut the plain cake into two pieces. _____, beat the cream until it is thick. _____, put one of the pieces of cake on a large plate and put half of the strawberries and half of the cream on top. _____, put the other piece on top of the cream. Repeat the layers of strawberries and cream. _____, put a few whole strawberries on top.

READING SKILLS

Scanning   Look at the newspaper advertisement that follows and mark the sentences TRUE or FALSE. Correct the false statements.

1. _____ The Berry Patch is the name of a business.

2. _____ The Berry Patch sells strawberries all summer.

3. _____ You can pick your own fruit at the Berry Patch.

4. _____ You must bring your own container with you.

5. _____ The Berry Patch is open every day.

6. _____ Strawberries you pick will cost you 65¢ for each pound.

7. _____ If you pick 100 pounds (45.5 kg) of strawberries, you will pay less than 65¢ a pound.

Pick Your Own Fruit
STRAWBERRIES — AVAILABLE
JUNE 5–30
(Container Provided)

65¢ per lb
50¢ for 25 lb or more

Open 7 A.M. to 7 P.M. Weekdays
THE BERRY PATCH
3 Miles South of Columbus
on Highway 62
(Closed Sundays)

lb = pound

CHAPTER REVIEW   List some reasons for picking your own fruit:

1. _____

2. _____

3. _____

4. _____

POST-READING ACTIVITIES

Word Game   The words on the right each contain the letters IN. Read the clues on the left and complete the words on the right.

Example

a store or factory   B U S I N E S S

1. to use your voice with music   _ I N _

2. to locate   _ I N _

3. an item   _ _ I N _

4. what you are doing on a horse   _ _ _ I N _

5. the largest meal of the day   _ I N _ _ _

6. *National Geographic*   _ _ _ _ _ I N _

7. 60 seconds   _ I N _ _ _

8. a season   _ I N _ _ _

9. to end   _ I N _ _ _

Crossword Puzzle

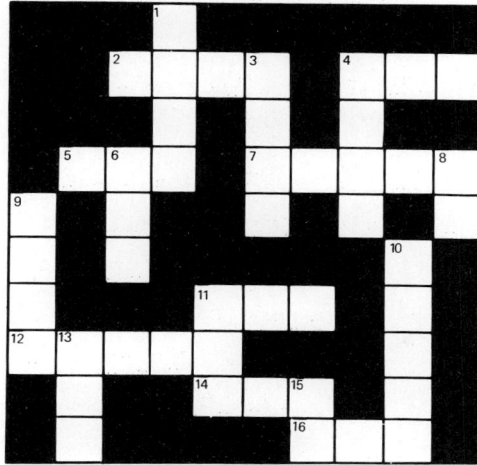

Across

2. the opposite of bad
4. the opposite of happy
5. the opposite of near
7. the opposite of right
11. the opposite of old
12. the opposite of here
14. the opposite of lose
16. the opposite of in

Down

1. the opposite of rich
3. the opposite of up
4. the opposite of fast
6. the opposite of to
   answer is to _____
8. the opposite of stop
9. the opposite of worst
10. the opposite of last
11. the opposite of used
13. the opposite of cold
15. the opposite of yes

Brooklyn Celebrates Labor Day

làm lễ; chúc tụng

PRE-READING

chức tước   *giáo hội*

Look at the title of this chapter and the picture on the left. Then decide the answers to these questions:

quyết định

1. What are the people doing?
2. Why are they dressed as they are?

45

READING 1

Scan the passage to find the answers to these questions:

1. What holiday do people in the United States celebrate in early September?
2. What part of New York has many West Indians?
3. How long is the parade route?

Read the passage carefully to learn the answer to this question:

How do West Indians celebrate Labor Day in the United States?

Float

Shark

¹ In early September, people in the United States celebrate Labor   1
Day. It is a day to remember workers. It is also the last summer
holiday. Many people go on picnics on this day. Other people relax
at home, watch a parade, or take part in a festival or celebration.

² In Brooklyn, an area of New York City, there is a special festival   5
on Labor Day. Brooklyn has a large West Indian population. On
Labor Day, these people from the Dominican Republic, Haiti,
Jamaica, Barbados, and Trinidad celebrate with music, dancing, special costumes and floats,° and special food and drink.

³ In the street you can hear the sound of steel drums. The drum-   10
mers are playing typical West Indian music. There is music from
Jamaica called reggae, music from Haiti called calypso, and music
from the Dominican Republic called merengue. There is music from
Barbados and Trinidad too. This music is playing very loudly from
buildings. People in the street are dancing to it.   15

⁴ As you walk along the street, you can smell food cooking. You can
see some people standing along the street. These people are selling
special West Indian food such as shark° steak from Jamaica. Many
people are drinking malt liquor with the food. Malt liquor is similar
to beer and very popular in the West Indies.   20

⁵ But West Indian carnivals are more than music, dancing, food,
and drink. People come to watch or take part in the parade. The
parade begins in the West Indian neighborhood of south-central
Brooklyn and continues for 2 miles (3.22 km). No cars are allowed on
the streets that day. Instead of cars, there are giant° floats. People   25
build and decorate the floats night and day for many weeks before
Labor Day. Each neighborhood tries to build the best float. Dancers
usually ride on the floats. These dancers are often pretty young
women in colorful costumes.

⁶ Other people dress in special costumes and walk along the pa- 30
rade route. People work very hard to make the costumes for the
Labor Day parade. Most of them are expensive and beautiful. Some
of the costumes are made of thousands of feathers° and take weeks
to sew. Some are funny. Others have a social message. For example,
one year a man dressed as a baby and rode in a baby carriage.° Instead 35
of milk, he was drinking a bottle of liquor. People saw the man and
laughed, but they also remembered the problems of West Indians in
the United States. Many West Indians are poor and have hard lives.
Some West Indians drink liquor because they want to forget their
troubles. Today liquor is a problem in West Indian society. The 40
Brooklyn celebration does not forget such problems.

⁷ So, the festival is a time for music, dancing, food, and drink, but
it is more than a day of fun. It is a time for West Indians in Brooklyn
to remember their old home far away and the problems of their new
home in the United States. 45

Feather

Baby carriage

COMPREHENSION CHECK

General Questions

Mark these statements TRUE or FALSE. Correct the false statements. Don't look back at the passage.

1. __F__ People in the United States celebrate Labor Day in May.

2. __T__ Labor Day is the first holiday of the summer.

3. __T__ Some Americans relax at home on Labor Day.

4. __T__ Brooklyn is part of New York City.

5. __T__ Malt liquor is like beer.

6. __F__ Most of the festival costumes are inexpensive.

7. __F__ The festival is only for fun.

Factual Questions

Answer these questions. You may look back at the passage.

1. What holiday do Americans celebrate in early September?
2. What do people do on this day?
3. What happens on Labor Day in Brooklyn?
4. How do West Indians celebrate on this day?

5. What kind of music is there at the carnival?
6. What foods do people eat at the carnival?
7. What kind of drink is popular?
8. What kind of costumes are there? What are some of the costumes made of?

** Inferential Questions Answer these questions. Read the passage again if necessary.

1. Why do people in Brooklyn play typical West Indian music on Labor Day?
2. Some people sell food at the Brooklyn celebration. Who cooks this food?
3. Why did the man dress as a baby and carry a bottle of liquor?
4. Where are West Indians from?

What Do You Think? 1. Is there a celebration in your town similar to the Brooklyn Labor Day parade? What day or event is celebrated? Are there costumes, special food and drink, and floats?
2. Would you like to attend the Brooklyn parade? Why or why not?
3. Are festivals necessary for people? Why or why not?

VOCABULARY SKILLS

Word Search 1. Write the word in line 6 that means *the number of people living in an area.*

_____

2. Write the word in line 9 that means *special or unusual dress.*

_____

3. Write the word in line 10 that means *a kind of metal.*

_____

4. Write the word in line 11 that means *usual.*

_____

5. Write the word in line 19 that means *like.*

_____

6. Write the word in line 26 that means *make beautiful.*

_____

7. Write the word in line 31 that means *the way from one place to another.*

_____

Idioms and Expressions   *to take part in*

Examples

1. She likes to participate in sports. She *takes part in* tennis, volleyball, and swimming.
2. My grandfather *took part in* World War II.
3. I like to watch parades, but I don't like to *take part in* them.

Give examples of activities that you take part in:

_____

_____

_____

Opposites   Fill in the blanks with the appropriate word:

1. (loudly/softly)   Many West Indians prefer to play music so everyone can hear it, but most old people like to play music *softly*.

2. (first/last)   In the United States, Memorial Day is at the beginning of summer. Labor Day in September is the _____ summer holiday.

3. (buy/sell)   Some people stand in the street and cook West Indian food. They ask if we want some. Are you hungry? We can _____ some food.

4. (night/day)   Most people work from morning to evening

and sleep at _____.

5. (forget/remember)   Don't _____! Labor Day is next

week, and I'll have a party.

Word Families   dance (noun)   We went to a *dance* last night.
dancing (noun)   *Dancing* is fun.
I went to *dancing* school.

dancer (noun-person)   I want to become a *dancer*.
dance (verb)   I like to *dance*. We *danced* all night.
danced
dancing

Use the listed words to fill in the blanks:

Do you want to learn how to _____? In most towns you can

choose from many kinds of _____ lessons. You can learn to

_____ the waltz or the rumba. You can learn to be a ballet

or tap _____. Best of all, the next time you go to a

_____, you'll be able to take part in the fun.

✱✱ Vocabulary in   take(s) part in   typical   watch
Context   celebrates   route   sell
parade

Use the listed words to fill in the blanks:

Every year on the 4th of July, our town *celebrates*. Most people

want to be in the parade. Part of this celebration includes a

_____. In fact, nearly everyone in town _____ it. There is really nothing unusual. It is a _____ American parade with loud music and floats. Some people sit along Main Street, the parade _____, and _____ the colorful floats. A few people _____ soft drinks and hot dogs.

READING SKILLS

Sentence Splitting Breaking long sentences down to short ones can help your reading comprehension. Follow these examples:

> Instead of cars, there are floats.
> *There aren't cars. There are floats.*
> They are playing reggae instead of jazz.
> *They are playing reggae. They aren't playing jazz.*

1. Instead of beer, there are soft drinks.

_____

2. Instead of singing, there is dancing.

_____

3. Instead of floats, there are bands.

_____

4. People eat shark steak instead of hot dogs.

_____

5. They are singing instead of watching TV.

_____

6. We picked strawberries instead of apples.

_____

7. Some people play soccer instead of football.

_____

Now look at this example:

> Other people relax at home, watch a parade, or take part in a festival.

The sentence contains three sentences:

1. Other people relax at home.
2. Other people watch a parade.
3. Other people take part in a festival.

Split the following sentences:

A. They celebrate with music, dancing, special costumes and floats, and special food and drink.

1. _____
2. _____
3. _____
4. _____

B. There is music from Jamaica called reggae and from Haiti called calypso.

1. _____
2. _____

C. Malt liquor is similar to beer and is very popular in the West Indies.

1. _____
2. _____

Main Ideas   Choose the main idea. The main idea of

1. paragraph 1 is:
   a. Labor Day is the last summer holiday.
   b. People go on picnics.
   c. There are many holidays in the United States.

2. paragraph 3 is:
   a. People are playing steel drums.
   b. People play West Indian music.
   c. There is music.

3. paragraph 4 is:
   a. People eat shark steak.
   b. People cook food.
   c. People sell and eat West Indian food.

4. paragraph 5 is:
   a. Pretty women in colorful costumes dance on the floats.
   b. The parade is an important part of the festival.
   c. West Indians have fun on Labor Day.

5. the whole passage is:
   a. This celebration serves many needs of the West Indians in Brooklyn.
   b. West Indians enjoy special costumes and parades on Labor Day.
   c. People in the United States celebrate Labor Day in many different ways.

READING 2

Read the invitation to learn the answers to these questions:

1. When is the picnic?
2. Where will it be?

R.S.V.P. = please answer "yes" or "no" to the invitation

AN INVITATION

*You are invited to
a Labor Day Picnic
on Monday, September 3
at 5:00* P.M.

Ted and Jane's
312 15th Street

R.S.V.P.
525-0923

Read the menu to learn the answers to these questions:

1. What kind of meat will there be?
2. How many salads will there be?

Ted and Jane's Menu
for Their Labor Day Picnic

barbecued chicken
potato salad
baked beans
green salad
rolls and butter
soft drinks
homemade ice cream
Ted's Chocolate Cake
coffee

Read Ted's Chocolate Cake recipe to learn the answers to these questions:

1. How many eggs does the recipe use?
2. How long does the cake have to bake?

Ted's Chocolate Cake Recipe

1. Open a chocolate cake mix.
2. Add $1\frac{1}{4}$ cup (296 ml) water.
3. Add 2 eggs.
4. Mix for 3 minutes.
5. Pour in pans.
6. Bake 25 minutes at 350°F (176.7°C).
7. Cool cake in pans for 10 minutes.
8. Remove from pans.
9. Frost cake with Jane's frosting.

COMPREHENSION CHECK

Answer these questions. You may look back to the invitation, menu, or recipe.

1. Who is giving the picnic?
2. Where will it be?
3. If you want to go to this picnic, what should you do?
4. When should you arrive at Ted and Jane's?
5. What are Ted and Jane serving as the main dish?
6. What kind of salads are they going to have?
7. What will the dessert be?
8. About how long will it take for Ted to make his cake?
9. What will Ted put on top of the finished cake?
10. Who will make the frosting for the cake?

READING SKILLS

Scanning

Ted and Jane will need to buy groceries for their party. Scan their menu and check the items on the list that they will probably need. Cross out items they won't need for the party. Follow the examples for the first two items.

1. chicken
2. ~~hamburger~~
3. fish
4. potatoes
5. lettuce
6. cucumbers
7. cans of baked beans
8. rolls
9. butter
10. beer
11. Coke
12. 7-Up
13. ice cream
14. cream
15. sugar
16. coffee
17. tea
18. chocolate cake mix
19. eggs

∗∗ Vocabulary in Context

in front of
right
around
on
after
along
over
left
at
before

After studying the map, fill in the blanks with the appropriate word:

The parade will begin at Ray's Garage (1) _on_ First Street. The floats will go (2) _along_ First Street and then go (3) _over_ the Yellow River. (4) _after_ they cross the Yellow River Bridge, they will go past the Sheldon Hotel. After that, they will go (5) _left_ on Main Street. They will pass Burn's Hardware and Daisy's Coffee Shop (6) _before_ they pass Paul's Grocery. Paul's Grocery is (7) _at_ the corner of Main and Eisenhower. The floats will turn (8) _right_ on Eisenhower Street, then go (9) _around_ the block. The parade will end (10) _____ the library.

CHAPTER REVIEW

1. List five possible Labor Day activities:

_____
_____
_____
_____
_____

2. List five activities at the Brooklyn Labor Day carnival:

_____
_____
_____
_____
_____

POST-READING ACTIVITIES

Word Find Puzzle   There are about 15 words in this puzzle. Begin with the letter *S* and go in the direction of the arrows. Write the words on the lines that follow.

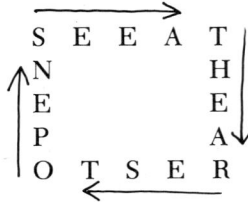

```
          →
   S  E  E  A  T |
 ↑ N           H |
   E           E |
   P           A ↓
 | O  T  S  E  R
        ←
```

see _____ _____ _____

eat _____ _____ _____

_____ _____ _____

_____ _____ _____

_____ _____ _____

Word Search Puzzle   Look at the list of U.S. holidays in the left column. Find these holidays in the word puzzle on the right and circle them. The words can go forward, backward, up, or down.

Christmas
Columbus Day
Easter
Halloween
Independence Day
Labor Day
Memorial Day
Mother's Day
New Year's Eve
Thanksgiving
Valentine's Day

```
N E W Y E A R S E V E V A H S
D E A R Y S L O G A H T R A P
E Y A D S U B M U L O C B L A
P N W E R V L N I E E D Y L E
E S T R X L O V M N O R I O L
N A R O L A B Y D T H L O W E
D M N S Y A D L A I R O M E M
G T I A Y P Y R A N L A B E R
I S S M O M E R X E S T R N E
U I H G N I V I G S K N A H T
I R S Q L A B O R D A Y E A S
N H T U U B H A P A F O D L A
G C H A S O A R I Y E A R O E
S A I T R Y A D S R E H T O M
I N D E P E N D E N C E D A Y
```

Clowns in Competition

PRE-READING

What are the men in the picture doing?
What sport are the men playing?
Do basketball players usually kick the ball into the basket?

61

READING 1

Scan the passage to find the answers to these questions:

1. What is the name of the basketball team?
2. What was the score near the end of the game?

Read the passage carefully to learn the answer to this question:

Why do these basketball players act like clowns?

Striped

Clown

¹ Five black basketball players run onto the court before the game. They are wearing red- and white-striped ° shorts and blue shirts with gold stars.

² The team begins to practice before the game. They make a circle and practice passing the ball. The players pass the ball over their heads or behind their backs. They play tricks, act like clowns,° and have a lot of fun.

³ During the game they also have fun. Players pass the ball between their legs and the legs of the other players. Sometimes they hit the ball with their heads and knees. Some players kick the ball into the basket. Are they playing basketball or football?

⁴ Sometimes one player keeps the ball for a long time. He dribbles the ball around the court. What are the other players doing? They are sitting on the floor playing cards.

⁵ These clowns in competition are the Harlem Globetrotters, the funniest and most famous basketball team in the world. At first the Globetrotters played only serious basketball. Then one day they were playing a team in a small town. The players on the other team were big, strong, and white, but they did not play basketball very well. Near the end of the game, the Globetrotters were winning 112 to 5.

⁶ The spectators began to get angry because their team was losing. They began to shout and throw things. The Globetrotters didn't want a fight, so they decided to act like clowns and make the spectators laugh. People cannot be angry and laugh at the same time.

⁷ The Globetrotters danced a little, passed the ball through their legs, and played other tricks. The spectators started to laugh and shout for more tricks.

⁸ That was just the beginning. Over the years the Globetrotters began to play more and more tricks. Now they almost never play serious basketball. They are a professional team, but their games are mainly funny shows to make spectators laugh. The spectators *do* laugh, but they also see some great basketball.

1

5

10

15

20

25

30

COMPREHENSION CHECK

General Questions

Mark these statements TRUE or FALSE. Correct the false statements. Don't look back at the passage.

1. _____ The team wears striped shorts.

2. _____ The team acts like clowns.

3. _____ The team plays soccer.

4. _____ The Harlem Globetrotters are very famous.

5. _____ The Globetrotters started to act like clowns because they were losing.

Factual Questions

Answer these questions. You may look back at the passage.

1. What kind of uniform do the players wear?
2. How do they pass the ball during practice?
3. What kind of basketball did the Globetrotters play at first?
4. Why was the other team losing the game?
5. Why were the spectators getting angry?
6. How did the Globetrotters make the spectators laugh?

** Inferential Questions

Answer these questions. Read the passage again if necessary.

1. Why do people like to watch the Globetrotters?
2. Why do the Globetrotters continue to act like clowns?

What Do You Think?

1. There are many competition sports. Which competition sport is most popular in your country?
2. What is your favorite sport? Are you a spectator or a participant in that sport?
3. Where do you usually find clowns? How are clowns different from ordinary people?

etc. = and others like these

4. What kind of card games do you like to play: poker, bridge, etc.?

VOCABULARY SKILLS

Word Search

1. Write the word in line 2 that means *having lines of different colors.*

   _____

2. Write the word in line 6 that means *playful jokes.*

   _____

3. Write the word in line 17 that means *not funny.*

   _____

4. Write the word on line 23 that means *give a loud cry.*

   _____

5. Write the word in line 24 that means *people watching.*

   _____

6. Write the word in line 31 that means *participating in a sport for money.*

   _____

Opposites   Fill in the blanks with the appropriate word:

(amateur/professional)

1. John McEnroe plays tennis. He plays in many competitions and usually wins a lot of money. He is a/an _____ tennis player.

(losing/winning)

2. Ray's team has 17 points, and the other team has 35 points. Ray's team is _____.

(over/under)

3. The child threw the ball _____ his head and out the window.

(always/never) 4. It almost _____ snows in Florida.

(a little/a lot) 5. Bill ate two eggs, bacon, toast, cereal, a few doughnuts, orange juice, milk, and coffee. Bill ate _____.

Word Families competition (noun) Most professional sports have *competitions*.
competitor (noun) Most professional *competitors* are famous.
compete (verb) People *compete* to win money and to become
   competed the best.
   competing

Use the listed words to fill in the blanks:

John Carmody plays tennis. He _____ in 20 games last year. He wants to _____ in more games this year. Next year he wants to participate in a national tennis _____. John is a good _____. He plays well, and he doesn't get angry on the court and throw things. It will be hard for John to win a _____ with famous _____, but he says he wants to try.

READING SKILLS

Main Ideas Choose the main idea. The main idea of

1. paragraph 2 is:
   a. The players practice before the game.
   b. The players pass the ball.
   c. The players play tricks and have a lot of fun during practice.

2. paragraph 6 is:
   a. The small town team was losing.
   b. The Globetrotters began to play tricks to stop a possible fight.
   c. The spectators began to shout and throw things.

3. paragraph 8 is:
   a. The Globetrotters mix great basketball with fun.
   b. It was just the beginning.
   c. The Globetrotters are a professional team.

4. the whole passage is:
   a. The Globetrotters play basketball.
   b. The Globetrotters are famous because they play funny tricks.
   c. The Globetrotters played serious basketball at first.

READING 2

Read the passage carefully to learn the history of the Harlem Globetrotters.

The Winning Team

Many years ago, in 1927, there was a black basketball team in   1
Chicago. The team needed a coach, so a man named Abe Saperstein
started to coach them. At first people laughed at this basketball team
because the players were tall and thin, and the coach was short and
round.°   5

However, by 1938, people were not laughing any more. From
1927 to 1938, Abe did three things for his team. He changed their
name to the Harlem Globetrotters. He also changed their uniform.
He made them the best and the most famous team in the country.

In the beginning Abe and his team had many problems. The most   10
important one was money. In those days professional teams got most
of their money from the sale of game tickets. If a lot of spectators
came to the game, then the players got a lot of money. However, only
a few people came to watch the Globetrotters play. So Abe and his
team decided to leave Chicago and travel to small towns to play   15
other teams.

The small towns were a problem, too. Players did not have good
gymnasiums to play in. The Globetrotters played many games in
dance halls or in church or high school gymnasiums. One time, in
Montana, they played basketball in a swimming pool. Of course, the 20

Short and round

Uphill and downhill

pool was empty, but the two teams had to run uphill and down-hill.°

Church gymnasiums and swimming pools did not bother the Globetrotters very much because they usually won. During their first basketball season (1927), they won 101 games and lost only 6. By 1938, they were the most famous basketball team because they had won so many games. 25

In 1940, the Globetrotters won the World Professional Basketball Tournament in Chicago. In 1950, they played 18 games with the best college players in the country and won 13 of those 18 games. 30

After 1950, the Globetrotters became famous in other countries, and in 1952, they went on their first tour around the world. Every year after that, they played in different countries in Europe and in Asia. Then, in 1970, they played their 10,000th game.

Today the team is still popular. They still travel around the world, 35 and spectators still like to watch them play and watch them win.

COMPREHENSION CHECK

Answer these questions. You may look back at the passage.

1. When did Abe Saperstein start to coach his team?
2. Why did people laugh at his team?
3. Where did the Globetrotters travel at first?
4. Where did small-town basketball teams usually play?
5. Where did the Globetrotters play in Montana?
6. How many games did the team win during their first season?
7. Why were they the most famous basketball team by 1938?
8. How many games did the team win in 1950?
9. Where does the team travel today?

VOCABULARY SKILLS

Matching Meanings The italicized words have more than one meaning. Match the correct meaning with each sentence:

A. a famous actor or actress   B. a light in the sky at night

__ 1. Who is your favorite movie *star?*

__ 2. You cannot see many *stars* tonight. It's cloudy.

__ 3. Tony wants to become a big *star.*

A. throw   B. complete successfully

__ 4. One player *passed* the ball to another player.

__ 5. Alice *passed* her examination.

__ 6. Will everyone *pass* the English course?

A. work   B. go quickly

__ 7. John had to *run* all the way home.

__ 8. That old washing machine doesn't *run* anymore.

__ 9. Is your watch *running?*

A. take part in   B. a performance
   a game or sport   in the theater

__ 10. What would you like to *play?*

__ 11. The *play* last night was good.

__ 12. The children *played* in the park.

A. performance   B. teach

__ 13. Will you *show* me how to make strawberry shortcake?

__ 14. The Globetrotters put on a good *show.*

__ 15. Chris didn't *show* me how to turn on the computer.

** Vocabulary in Context

behind   shouts   striped   uniform
clowns   spectators   tricks

Fill in the blanks with the appropriate word:

Here come the _____, the funniest people in the circus. The _____ watch the clowns and laugh at their funny _____. One big clown is wearing _____ pants, and a short clown is wearing a policeman's _____. The big clown has a little dog. The little dog runs _____ the short clown and tries to bite him. The little clown _____ loudly and tries to run away.

READING SKILLS

Connecting Words   *however* = but

Example

The Globetrotters became famous. *However,* in the beginning they had many problems.

Complete these sentences:

1. I like music. However, I don't like _____ _____.

2. The Globetrotters can play serious basketball. However, most of the time they _____.

3. Many schools have computers. However, the students _____.

4. Many camps have special programs. However, most camps still

have _____.

5. That old lady looks poor. However, she has _____

_____.

6. Playing soccer is an outdoor activity. However, watching TV is

_____.

Scanning

STATE UNIVERSITY
vs
POLYTECH
Sat., Oct. 2, 1982
1:30 P.M.

POLYTECH
3 EE 1 04
Gate Sec. Row Seat
South Field Bleacher
ADMIT ONE
$10.00
State Tax Included

South Field Bleacher
ADMIT ONE
$10.00
State Tax Included
Gate Sec. Row Seat
3 EE 1 04
POLYTECH

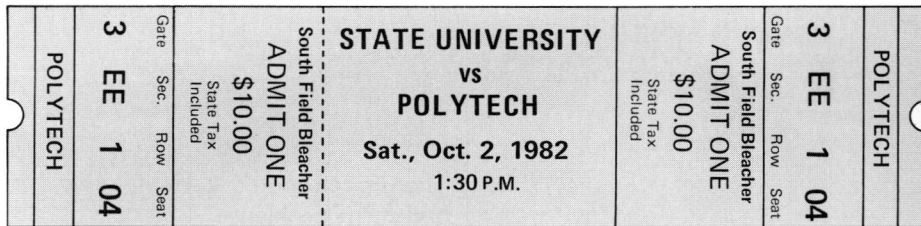

Look at this football ticket. Scan it to find the answers to these
questions:

1. What two teams are playing?
2. When does the game begin?
3. What is the price of the ticket?
4. Does this ticket include tax?
5. What side of the field will you be sitting on?
6. What gate should you go in?
7. What section will you be sitting in?
8. What row will you be sitting in?

CHAPTER REVIEW

1. Describe the Harlem Globetrotters.

   _____

   _____

2. Describe the kind of basketball they play.

   _____

   _____

3. Explain why they are the most famous basketball team in the world.

   _____

   _____

POST-READING ACTIVITIES

Word Game   The words in the right column each contain the letters ON. Read the clues in the left column and complete the words on the right.

Example

_____, two, three   O N <u>*E*</u>

1. you buy things with this   __ O N __ __
2. one time   O N __ __
3. 12 o'clock   __ __ O N
4. you eat soup with this   __ __ __ O N
5. schools are closed during _____   __ __ __ __ __ __ O N
6. not weak   __ __ __ O N __
7. first, _____, third   __ __ __ O N __
8. winter is a _____   __ __ __ __ O N

Crossword Puzzle

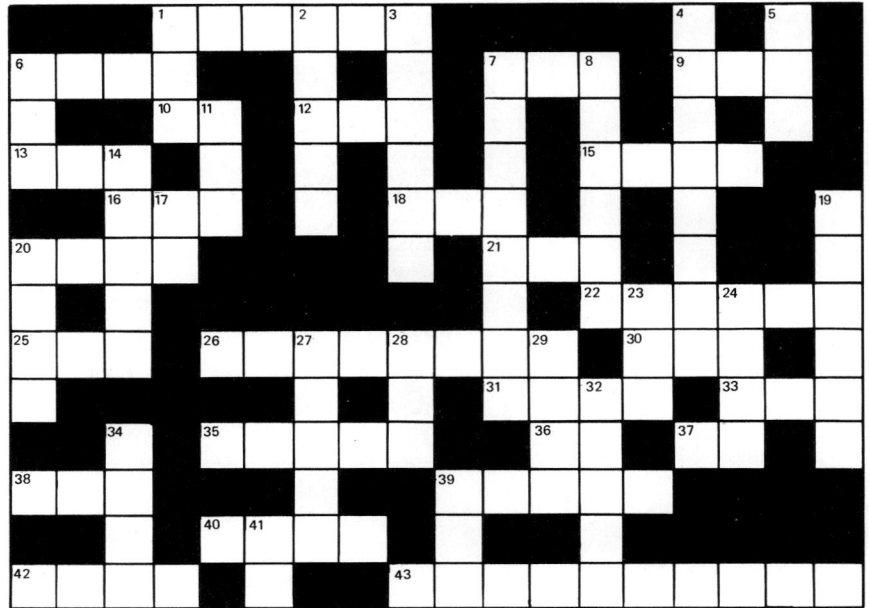

Across

1. a kind of football game
6. what your foot does with a ball
7. This gift is ___ you.
9. not lose; but ___
10. not out; but __
12. bread ___ butter
13. not no; but ___
15. ___ in and sit down
16. you cook in it
18. you need this to play volleyball
20. not rich; but ___
21. it makes honey
22. you need a net, a racket, and a ball to play this
25. not stand; but ___
26. a popular U.S. summer team sport
30. five years ___
31. not won; but ___
33. look

35. where you play tennis or basketball
36. not down; but __
37. you and I
38. also
39. this day
40. two points for a soccer ___
42. a grass sport played with clubs
43. this sport uses a net

Down

1. you can do this in winter
2. he helps the team
3. what you're doing on a horse
4. a water sport
5. not begin; but ___
6. you need this to start the car
7. an American sport

8. what you need to play tennis
11. Golf is ___ a team sport
14. baseball is a _____
17. you can spend __ save your money
19. you need this to pick strawberries
20. throw or kick the ball to a teammate

23. let's ___ dinner
24. you smell with this
27. an underwater sport
28. you hit a ball with this
29. not soft music; but ____ music
32. a place where astronauts work
34. a place for swimming
39. one, ___, three
41. not off; but __

6

A Different Kind of House

PRE-READING

Compare the two houses.
How are they alike and how are they different?
Which house do you prefer? Why?

75

READING 1

Scan the passage to find the answers to these questions:

1. How much did the couple pay for the old train station?
2. How many people are there in the Illinois family?

Now read the passage carefully to learn the answers to these questions:

1. What do some people do with old buildings?
2. What kind of building did the Illinois family buy?

Bricks
Gạch

¹ There are many different kinds of houses in the United States. 1
They can be large or small, old or modern, or anything in between.
Many houses are square, and a few are round. Some have basements,
and some do not. Some houses have only one floor, and others have
two or more. Most houses are made of concrete, wood, stone, or 5
bricks.°   *Bê tông*   *đá*

² Many old houses need a lot of repair work. The owners may
repair or rebuild the houses themselves. Sometimes homeowners
only need to redecorate. Other times they design a new kitchen or
tân trí
bathroom, or even add a whole new floor. 10

³ A few people are not happy with any of these houses. These
people buy old buildings, such as old banks, churches, schools, or gas
stations. They spend a lot of time and money to change these old
buildings into homes, but they can say, "My home is different." 15

⁴ People in different parts of the United States are buying old
buildings and changing them into homes. A woman in San Francisco
converted an old wooden church into a home. A couple in Massachusetts bought an old train station for $1000 and changed it into a
home. Two women in California bought two old train cars. They 20
changed one into a store and the other into their home.

⁵ One family in Illinois wanted a small house for the summer. They
saw a small farm building in a cornfield. Farmers usually store their
corn in these buildings, but the Illinois family wanted one for their
summer home. They bought it and converted it to a comfortable 25
house for the summer.

⁶ They put new windows on the sides. The windows keep the little
house cool during the hot summer. They also put in a kitchen, bath,
and stairs. On the second floor, they put in two small bedrooms. On
the first floor, they put in another bedroom. Now all 9 people live 30
comfortably in their small summer house.

COMPREHENSION CHECK

General Questions

Mark these statements TRUE or FALSE. Correct the false statements. Don't look back at the passage.

1. _____ All houses have basements.

2. _____ Some owners like to add new rooms to their houses.

3. _____ A few people are not happy with the usual kinds of houses.

4. _____ A few people convert old buildings to houses.

5. _____ One Illinois family wanted a small winter house.

6. __T__ The Illinois family changed a farm building into a house.

Factual Questions

Answer these questions. You may look back at the passage.

1. What are some houses made of?
2. What do some owners do with their houses?
3. What kinds of old buildings do a few people buy?
4. What did the woman in San Francisco buy?
5. What did the two women in California do with the two old train cars?
6. Why did the Illinois family put windows on the sides?
7. What rooms did they add?
8. How many bedrooms does the little house have?

**Inferential Questions

Answer these questions. Read the passage again if necessary.

1. Why do some people want to change old buildings into houses?
2. What are some problems with changing old buildings into houses?
3. Where is the summer house?

What Do You Think?

1. Compare homes in your country to homes in the United States?
2. What do people in your country do with old houses, cars, or TV sets? Do they rebuild or repair them? Do they throw them away?
3. Would people in your country change an old building such as a bank into a home? Why or why not?

VOCABULARY SKILLS

Word Search

1. Write the word in line 3 that means *like a circle.*

   _____

2. Write the word in line 5 that means *something that comes from trees.*

   _____

3. Write the word in line 8 that means *fix.*

   _____

4. Write the word in line 8 that means *build again.*

   _____

5. Write the word in line 23 that means *keep for the future.*

   _____

Idioms and Expressions

made of

Look at these examples:

1. Some houses are *made of* concrete.
2. A bottle is *made of* glass.
3. This dress is *made of* cotton.

Answer these questions:

1. What are houses in your country made of?
2. What is your shirt made of?
3. What is made of metal and glass and has four wheels and a motor?

spend

We use the word *spend* with words such as *time, money,* and *energy.*

Examples

1. Rich people can *spend* a lot of money.
2. Parents like to *spend* time with their children.
3. He *spends* a lot of time and energy helping other people.

The OPPOSITE of *spend* is the word *save*.

Examples

1. You can *save* money in a bank.
2. Do your homework carefully. You can *save* time this way. You won't have to write it again.
3. *Save* energy! Turn off a light.

Use the words *save* or *spend* in these sentences:

1. Some people never use a bank. They _____ their money in a steel box at home.
2. John keeps his apartment cool in winter. He says this _____ energy.
3. Families like to _____ time together.
4. John sleeps in his clothes. He doesn't have to dress in the morning. This _____ him a lot of time.
5. Mary likes to _____ her free time watching TV.

Opposites   Fill in the blanks with the appropriate word:

(different/same)   1. My father's name is Jack Smith. My name is Jack Smith, too. My father and I have the _____ name.

(small/large)   2. The Johnsons' house has six bedrooms. It is a _____ house.

(comfortable/uncomfortable)   3. This chair is very _____. I can't sit here for a long time.

(cool/warm)   4. It's best to store milk in a _____ place.

(front/back)

5. John sits near the teacher. He sits in the _____ of the room.

(top/bottom)

6. Look at a clock. The number at the _____ of the clock is six.

READING SKILLS

Connecting Words   Look at this sentence:

I was hungry, *so* I made a sandwich.

We use the word *so* to connect sentences. The second sentence is a result of the first sentence.

Match the sentences in Column A with the sentences in Column B:

Column A	*Column B*
___ 1. We don't want this old coffee pot, so	a. they go to Bollay's camp.
___ 2. People don't like to throw away useful things, so	b. we can't go to the movies tonight.
___ 3. Some people want a different kind of house, so	c. let's add some windows.
___ 4. Some children want to combine fun with learning, so	d. they have a garage or yard sale.
___ 5. We don't have any money, so	e. let's throw it away.
___ 6. We want to keep our house cool during the summer, so	f. they buy old buildings and change them.

Sentence Splitting   Look at this example:

Most houses are made of concrete, wood, or bricks.

The sentence contains three sentences:

1. Most houses are made of concrete.
2. Most houses are made of wood.
3. Most houses are made of bricks.

Split the sentences below:

A. They can be large or small.

    1. _____

    2. _____

B. Some owners add a new bedroom, a new bathroom, or a new floor.

    1. _____

    2. _____

    3. _____

C. They are wearing red- and white-striped shorts and blue shirts with gold stars.

    1. _____

    2. _____

D. The team played games in dance halls, in churches, or in high school gymnasiums.

    1. _____

    2. _____

    3. _____

Main Ideas   Choose the main idea. The main idea of

1. paragraph 1 is:
   a. Some houses have basements.
   b. There are many different kinds of houses in the United States.
   c. Many people buy houses in the United States.

2. paragraph 3 is:
   a. Some people buy old buildings because they're not happy with typical houses.
   b. Some people spend a lot of money on their houses.
   c. People want a different kind of house.

3. paragraph 5 is:
   a. People want summer houses.
   b. One family wanted a summer house.
   c. Farmers have summer houses for their corn.

4. paragraph 6 is:
   a. The family bought a little house.
   b. The family put in rooms.
   c. The family made many changes in the little house.

READING 2

Read the passage to learn the answer to this question:

What may be the house of the future?

Some people like to live in houses of the past. They may choose   1
to live in a log house.° They say these houses are easy to build and
warm in winter. Others like to live in houses of the future. They may
live in a solar house. A solar house gets its energy from the sun.

A few other people like to live in houses combining the past and   5
the future. These people may live in a house under the ground. Many
people think underground houses are cold and dark, but that is not
true. These houses have special windows in the roof or large windows
on one side. These windows give the houses a lot of light.

The idea of underground houses is very old. People in the past   10
lived in underground houses and underground cities in China, Spain,
and Turkey. Today there are large underground shopping centers in
Japan, South Korea, and Canada. Some countries also build underground factories and storehouses to hold things.

In the United States, more people are beginning to build under-   15
ground houses. Underground houses save open land. When houses
are underground, there is more land for parks, tennis courts, and
gardens. Underground houses also save energy. They use only a little
energy to stay warm or cool.

Joyce Rinker has an underground house in Michigan. One day in   20
February, the outside temperature was a cold 8°F (−13.3°C), but the
temperature inside her house was 66°F (18.9°C). The next year, in
July, the outside temperature was a hot 93°F (33.9°C), but the temperature inside was a comfortable 72°F (22.2°C).

Log house

F = Fahrenheit
C = Celsius

Owners of underground houses like them. John Bonard is an archi- 25
tect. He designed an underground house in New England. His wife,
Barbara, is an outdoor person, but she likes her underground home.
"It's ideal. I love it," she says.

More and more people in the United States like the idea of living
underground. They are building more offices, schools, and houses 30
underground. Who knows? Perhaps in the future whole cities will be
underground.

COMPREHENSION CHECK

Answer these questions. You may look back at the passage.

1. Why do some people live in log houses?
2. Why aren't underground houses dark and cold?
3. Where did people live in underground cities?
4. What do some countries build underground?
5. Why do people want to save open land?
6. How do owners of underground houses feel about them?

VOCABULARY SKILLS

Opposites   Fill in the blanks with the appropriate word:

(dark/light)   1. The room is too _____. Turn on the lamp.

(easy/difficult)   2. Sue did not study last night. It will be _____ for her to pass the test.

(under/above)   3. Most houses today are _____ the ground.

(past/future)   4. Will people of the _____ live in underground cities?

(inside/outside)   5. You do not usually wear your coat _____.

Matching Meanings   Match the meaning with each sentence:

A. shop   B. keep for the future

___ 1. We went to the *store* for some fruit.

___ 2. Farmers *store* their corn in special buildings.

___ 3. You can buy almost anything at a *store*.

A. prefer   B. similar to

___ 4. John looks *like* his father.

___ 5. I *like* tea, not coffee.

___ 6. What would you *like* to drink?

A. bottom of a room   B. story of a building

___ 7. The *floor* is very dirty.

___ 8. Some people like to sit on the *floor*.

___ 9. We live on the second *floor*.

A. an area of study   B. farm area

___ 10. Farmer Brown is growing corn in that *field*.

___ 11. The horses are eating in the *field* next to the house.

___ 12. What is your *field*?

A. brightness   B. not heavy

___ 13. The rooms in the house have a lot of *light*.

___ 14. This paperback dictionary is easy to carry because it is *light*.

___ 15. Turn on the lamp. We need more *light*.

READING SKILLS

Choose the best meaning for each italicized word. Use the context
to help you.

1. Some countries build *storehouses* to hold things.
   a. special places to keep things
   b. special houses for stores
   c. special stores for houses

2. Underground houses save *open land* for parks, tennis courts, and
   gardens.
   a. land used for buildings
   b. land used for underground houses
   c. land not used for buildings

3. John Bonard is an *architect.* He designed an underground house
   in New England.
   a. a building designer
   b. an arch designer
   c. an underground-house designer.

Connections Look at these sentences from the passage:

Some houses have only one floor. <u>Others</u> have two or more.

others = houses

Connect the underlined words to the words they refer to:

1. They changed one train car into a store and changed the <u>other</u> into
   their home.

2. Farmers usually store their corn in these buildings, but the Illinois
   family wanted <u>one</u> for their summer home.

3. Some people like to live in houses of the past. <u>Others</u> like to live
   in houses of the future.

Scanning   Scan the newspaper ads to find the answers to these questions:

1. Which is the cheapest one-bedroom apartment?

2. Can you have a dog at the 44th and University apartment?

3. Which apartment doesn't allow children?

4. Which apartment is part of a house?

5. What is the address of the house with the most bedrooms?

6. Which house is near the university?

7. Which house has a garage?

8. Which house is cheapest to rent?

APARTMENTS FOR RENT	HOUSES FOR RENT
44th & University, newly remodeled house, 1 BR $250, 2BR $295. No pets. 254-4344	University Village, nice, clean, 2BR, lg LR and DR, crpt, w/gar and stove. No pets. 262-2368
38th & University, deluxe 2BR, large kit, heat and water pd., $315 quiet build. Adults 254-1174	3BR house near campus, din rm, liv rm, 2 children, $325 mo. Garbage and water pd. 267-2287
1826 9th, 1 BR, 2nd floor, clean, crpt., no pets, $160/mo. 252-5161	Comfortable 3–4 BR, full bath, parking. Avail now, $400 + deposit. 1442 11th

---

What do these abbreviations mean?

BR _____   w/gar _____

kit _____   crpt _____

bath _____   avail _____

pd _____   LR _____

bldg _____   lg _____

mo _____   DR _____

CHAPTER REVIEW

1. Describe different kinds of houses in the United States.

   _____

2. Tell something about underground homes.

   _____

3. Tell what underground houses save. Explain why.

   _____

   _____

POST-READING ACTIVITIES

Measurements

Distance

1 inch = 2.54 centimeters
1 foot = 30.48 centimeters
1 yard = 0.914 meters
1 mile = 1.609 kilometers

Area

1 acre = 0.4047 hectares

Weight

1 ounce = 28.35 grams
1 pound = 0.4536 kilograms

Answer these questions:

1. The West Indian parade route is 2 miles long. How many kilometers is that?

   _____

2. Mr. Furleigh has 28 acres of strawberries. How many hectares does he have?

   _____

3. How much do you weigh?

   In kilograms? _____

   In pounds? _____

Temperature

°C	°F
37.8	100
33.3	92
28.9	84
24.4	76
17.8	64

°C	°F
13.3	56
8.9	48
4.4	40
0	32

°C	°F
−1.1	20
−15.6	4
−20	−4
−24	−12

Answer these questions.

1. The temperature in February is −4°F. What is the temperature in Celsius?

   _____

2. The inside temperature is 64°F. What is the temperature in Celsius?

   _____

3. What is the highest temperature where you live?

   _____

   What is the lowest temperature where you live?

   _____

WORD GAME   Each word in the right column contains the letters OR. Read the clues in the left column and complete the words in the right.

Example

vocabulary   W O R D S

1. this gift is _____ you   _ O R

2. a job, for example   _ O R _

3. a yellow vegetable   _ O R _

4. you open a _____ to go in   _ _ O R

5. basketball is one   _ _ O R _

6. a place to buy things   _ _ O R _

7. an animal you ride   _ O R _ _

8. a story of a building   _ _ _ O R

9. what a team wears   _ _ _ _ O R _

10. a person living next door   _ _ _ _ _ _ O R

Learning, American Style: Boys and Babies

PRE-READING

Where do you think the boy and the baby in the picture are?
What are they doing?
Is there anything unusual about the picture?

READING 1

Scan the passage to find the answers to these questions:

1. How old are the boys in the babies class?
2. Where is Collegiate School?

Read the passage carefully to learn the answer to this question:

What kind of class is the babies class?

Diaper *tã lót*

Weight lifter
xiến cử nặg lên

¹ A group of boys 10 and 11 years old walk into a classroom at   1
Collegiate School. They hear babies crying. The boys are curious
about their new class. It is called "babies."

² The boys don't have to take the class. They are volunteers. The
babies are not dolls. They are real, live babies. The boys learn how   5
to feed, dress, wash, and carry them. They even learn how to change
diapers° and what to do in emergencies. Most of the boys have a good
time in the class. Some of them ask to take it again.

³ Collegiate is a private boys' school in New York. The boys take
required courses in math, English, social studies, and science. They   10
can also choose electives in weight lifting,° photography, kite flying,
and computer science. Recently, the principal at Collegiate decided
to try something different. He offered the boys a new elective. In the
class, the boys use real babies to learn about child care.

⁴ Where does the school get the babies? Mothers in the neighbor-   15
hood near the school volunteer their babies for a few hours each
week. These mothers like sharing their children with others.

⁵ The boys like the class very much, but the popularity of the class
surprises some adults. In some countries, like China or Israel, older
children often take care of younger children. However, in the United   20
States, this is not typical. Many older boys in the United States say it
is not masculine to take care of babies and young children. They say,
"Girls should take care of babies." Some parents say, "Taking care of
babies is too difficult for young boys." Yet, the Collegiate School class
is popular. Why?   25

Certificate *bằng cấp*
giấy chứng nhận

⁶ Maybe it is because these children are young and do not think that child care is only for girls. Maybe it is because children this age are curious about everything, including babies. Maybe it is because children in the United States about age 10 or 11 like to earn their own money. Baby-sitting is a good way for them to make a few dollars.   30

⁷ When the boys finish the babies course, they receive official certificates.° The certificates say the boys completed a course in child care. These may help the boys get baby-sitting jobs.

COMPREHENSION CHECK

General Questions

Mark these sentences TRUE or FALSE. Correct the false statements. Don't look back at the passage.

1. _____ Students at Collegiate take certain required courses.

2. _____ These students can choose certain elective classes.

3. _____ Math is an elective course at Collegiate School.

4. _____ The babies class isn't popular.

5. _____ In the United States, most young boys don't take care of babies.

6. _____ Some parents say, "Taking care of babies is too difficult for young boys."

7. _____ Baby-sitting is a way to make money.

Factual Questions

Answer these questions. You may look back at the passage.

1. Who is taking the new elective class?
2. What is the name of the class?
3. What do the students learn about babies in the class?
4. What other classes can the boys choose to take?
5. Why do the boys like the course?
6. How do children in the United States often earn money?
7. What do the boys receive after they complete the course?

** Inferential Questions   Answer these questions. Read the passage again if necessary.

1. Why does the popularity of the class surprise some adults?
2. Why do some boys say it is not masculine to take care of babies?
3. How might the certificates help the boys to get baby-sitting jobs?

What Do You Think?

1. Why do you think the babies class is popular?
2. Who takes care of babies and young children in your family? Women only? Both men and women? Older children? Relatives of the family? Friends?
3. Do 10- to 11-year-old children earn money in your home country? Are they expected to work around the house without pay? What is typical work for children in your home country?
4. Do older boys in your culture sometimes feel it is not masculine to take care of babies? Why do you think many boys in the United States feel this way?
5. Could there be a class like this one in your country? Would it be successful? Why or why not?
6. How do people learn how to take care of children and babies in your home country?

VOCABULARY SKILLS

Word Search

1. Write the word in line 2 that means *wanting to know more about something.*

   _____

2. Write the word in line 4 that means *persons who offer to do something.*

   _____

3. Write the word in line 7 that means *pants for a baby.*

   _____

4. Write the word in line 7 that means *dangerous situations that need immediate attention.*

   _____

5. Write the word in line 9 that is the opposite of *public.*

_____

6. Write the word in line 10 that means *something you must do.*

_____

7. Write the word in line 11 for *courses you do not have to take.*

_____

8. Write the word in line 12 for *the head of a school.*

_____

9. Write the word in line 17 that means *giving part of something that is yours to someone else.*

_____

Idioms and Expressions   *pick* = (1) harvest,   (2) choose

Examples

1. The corn is ready to *pick.*
2. Please *pick* a date for the party.

pick up = (1) lift,   (2) get

Examples

1. *Pick up* the baby.
2. *Pick* me *up* at eight.

Use *pick* or *pick up* in the blanks:

1. The fruit is ripe and ready to _____.

2. I'll _____ Karen after school, and we'll drive home.

3. Be careful when you _____ the baby.

4. The dresses are all so beautiful, I don't know which to

_____.

5. Be sure to _____ my suit at the cleaners on your way

home.

Opposites   Fill in the blanks with the appropriate word:

(artificial/real)   1. A doll is not a/an _____ baby.

(teach/learn)   2. The boys do not know how to wash babies. The
                          mothers _____ them how.

(private/public)   3. Some children go to a school like the Collegiate
                          School.   But   most   children   go   to   a
                          _____ school.

(give/receive)   4. After they finish the class, the boys will
                          _____ an official certificate from the
                          school.

Word Families   baby-sitting (noun)   *Baby-sitting* is a good way to earn
                                                 money.

                    baby-sitter (noun-person)   A *baby-sitter* takes care of children.

                    baby-sit (verb)   Boys or girls can *baby-sit.*
                      baby-sat
                      baby-sitting

Use the listed words to fill in the blanks:

Mr. and Mrs. Brown are going to the movies tonight. They need a

_____. They call Bob. Bob wants to earn some money. He

knows   how   to   _____.   Bob   says,   "Yes."   Bob   likes

_____.

photograph (noun)   Do you have *photographs* of the Col-
                               legiate School?

photography (noun)   *Photography* is not a typical class.

photographer (noun-person)   Mr. Smith is a *photographer.*

photograph (verb)   He is *photographing* the babies in
  photographed   the class.
  photographing

Use the listed words to fill in the blanks:

_____ is a popular class at Collegiate School. Mr. Byrd is a

_____. He is also the teacher of the class. The boys in the

class are taking only black-and-white _____. Now they

want to _____ the infants in the babies class.

** **Vocabulary in Context**

curious   earn   grade   crawling
popular   typical   group

Use the listed words to fill in the blanks:

Bob Smith is in the fifth _____. He is _____ about

the new babies class. Babies is not a _____ class for boys, but

it is a _____ class. Bob wants to _____ some

money. Maybe baby-sitting is a good way. Bob goes into the class-

room. On the floor is a _____ of babies. One baby is crying,

and another baby is _____ towards Bob.

READING SKILLS

Guessing Meanings from Context

Choose the best meaning for each italicized word.
Use the context to help you.

1. The boys don't have to take the class. They are *volunteers*.
   a. supporters
   b. soldiers
   c. people who offer to do something
   d. students who attend private schools

2. The boys take required courses in math, English, social studies,
   and science. They can also choose *electives* in weight lifting, photography, kite flying, and computer science.
   a. private courses
   b. required courses
   c. free courses
   d. courses students can choose

3. Many older boys in the United States say it is not *masculine* to take care of babies and young children. They say, "Girls should take care of babies."
   a. womanlike
   b. manlike
   c. childlike
   d. ladylike

4. Children in the United States about age 10 or 11 like to *earn* their own money. Baby-sitting is a good way for them to make a few dollars.
   a. make
   b. spend
   c. save
   d. keep

Connections   Look at this example:

Connect the underlined word or group of words to the idea they refer to.

The (Collegiate School class is popular.) Why? Maybe it is because these children are young and do not think that child care is only for girls.

it = Collegiate School class is popular

1. Recently, the principal at Collegiate School decided to try something new. He offered the boys <u>a new elective course called "babies."</u>

2. Most of the boys have a good time in the class. <u>Some of them</u> ask to take it again.

3. In some countries, like China or Israel, older children take care of younger children. However, in the United States, <u>this</u> is not typical.

4. The certificates say the boys completed a course in child care. <u>These</u> may help the boys get baby-sitting jobs.

Main Ideas Choose the main idea. The main idea of

1. paragraph 2 is:
   a. The boys learn about babies.
   b. The boys learn to change diapers.
   c. The boys enjoy learning how to take care of real babies.

2. paragraph 4 is:
   a. The school gets babies.
   b. Mothers of babies live in the neighborhood near the school.
   c. Mothers volunteer their babies for the class.

3. paragraph 5 is:
   a. The class is popular, but many people don't understand why.
   b. In some countries, older children take care of younger children.
   c. Many older boys in the United States say it is not masculine to take care of babies and young children.

4. the whole passage is:
   a. Mothers volunteer to share their babies.
   b. Children in the United States like to baby-sit.
   c. The child care class for boys is popular.

READING 2 Read the passage carefully to learn the answers to these questions:

1. Who is Ted?
2. What will the boys learn in the babies class?

Ted is a 10-year-old boy in the fifth grade at Collegiate School. He is standing outside a classroom. He is nervous about his new child care class.

He hears a baby crying behind the closed door. Ted's classmate walks by:

Bob: "What's that? It sounds like a baby crying."
Ted: "It is a baby. It's for our babies class."
Bob: "Gee, you mean you use real babies?"
Ted: "Yeah. We learn how to hold them, dress them, wash them, and change their diapers."
Bob: "Change diapers? Boy! You're in for trouble!"

Ted: "Hey, I have to go now. It's time for our class."

Ted enters the room with several other boys. Inside are five babies. One is crawling across the floor. Two others are sleeping in baby carriages.   15

Mrs. Mahrer is the teacher. She picks up one of the crying babies. "Ted, this is Carrie."

"Why is she crying?" asks Ted.

"She is unhappy because her mother is not here," answers Mrs. Mahrer.   20

Carrie stops crying. "Look, she likes you!" says Mrs. Mahrer. "Would you like to hold her?" She shows Ted how to hold the baby. "Put one hand under Carrie's bottom and the other hand behind her head. That's right. Now, why don't you try holding another baby?"

Mrs. Mahrer tells the boys about future classes. Next week they   25
will learn to diaper a baby. The third week they'll learn to feed a baby. The fourth week Mrs. Mahrer will show the class how to give a baby a bath. The fifth week the boys will learn to play with babies, and on the sixth week Mrs. Mahrer will talk to her class about dangers and emergencies. At the end of the course, each boy will receive a   30
certificate. It will say the boy is a good baby-sitter.

Adapted from *Ms.*

COMPREHENSION CHECK

Answer these questions. You may look back at the passage.

1. What does Ted hear?

2. How does Ted feel about his new class?

3. What are the babies doing inside the classroom?

4. Why is Carrie crying?

5. What does Mrs. Mahrer say is the way to hold a baby?

6. What will the boys learn in future babies classes?

7. What will the boys receive at the end of the course?

Vocabulary Skills **101**

VOCABULARY SKILLS

Idioms and Expressions   Look at this expression from the reading passage:

"*Why don't you* try holding another baby?"

WHY + DO + NOT + PRONOUN = { a suggestion in question form

Look at these examples:

TOM: Joe's tooth hurts.

MARY: *Why doesn't he* go to the dentist if he has a tooth-ache?

VIVIAN: I'm hungry.

BARBARA: *Why don't we* go have a hamburger?

Practice using this idiom by completing the second half of the following dialogues:

1. Jeff: I don't feel well.

   Daisy: _____

2. Jane: The weather is great, and I'm tired of studying.

   Fred: _____

3. Greg: I can't find my other shoe.

   Judy: _____

4. Bob: The baby is crying.

   Mrs. Mahrer: _____

5. Mary: John has trouble sleeping.

   Laura: _____

READING SKILLS

Scanning

		School Schedule			

Name _____Bob Smith_____   School _____Carver Elementary_____

Grade _____5_____   Teacher _____Mr. Wagner_____

Time	Monday	Tuesday	Wednesday	Thursday	Friday
9–10	Reading	Reading	Reading	Reading	Reading
10–11	Music	Physical Education	Music	Physical Education	Social Studies
11–12	Science	Library	Science	Art	Science
12–1	Lunch	Lunch	Lunch	Lunch	Lunch
1–2	English	English	Social Studies	English	English
2–3	Arithmetic	Arithmetic	Babies	Arithmetic	Arithmetic

Scan Bob's school schedule to learn the answers to these questions:

1. What school does Bob go to?
2. Who is his teacher?
3. When does school begin? When does it end?
4. When does Bob go to the library?
5. When does Bob eat lunch?
6. When does Bob have the babies class?
7. What class does Bob have from 9 to 10?

Write your class schedule here:

Time	Monday	Tuesday	Wednesday	Thursday	Friday

Class Schedule

Name: _____   Major: _____

University: _____   Term: _____

CHAPTER REVIEW

1. List things the boys learn in their babies class:

_____

_____

_____

_____

_____

_____

2. List reasons why these boys might like the babies class:

_____

_____

_____

_____

_____

POST-READING ACTIVITIES

This information may be important for you, a baby-sitter, or a visitor in your home:

Emergency information:

My name _____ _____

Address _____

Telephone numbers: home _____   work _____

In an emergency call:

Name _____

Address _____

Telephone numbers: home _____   work _____

Police _____

Fire department _____

Doctor _____

Ambulance service _____

NOTE: (Medical information) _____

_____

Double Trouble   All the words in the right column have double letters. Read the meanings in the left column and fill in the missing letters.

Example

a big meal   D I N N E R

1. not big   _ _ T T _ _

2. a snow sport   _ _ I I _ _

3. a kind of football game   _ _ C C _ _

4. 100 cents   _ _ L L _ _

5. what you put on toast   _ _ T T _ _

6. throws a ball   _ _ S S _ _

7. first person in a race   _ _ N N _ _

8. something you write to a friend   _ _ T T _ _

9. a court sport   _ _ N N _ _

10. the warmest season   _ _ M M _ _

11. he or she takes care of children   _ _ T T _ _

12. reading for specific information   _ _ _ N N _ _ _

Mickey, the Middle-Aged Mouse

PRE-READING

Compare the pictures of Mickey Mouse.
How are they alike and different?

READING 1

Scan the passage to find the answers to these questions:

1. When did Walt Disney and Ub Iwerks create Mickey Mouse?
2. How many films was Mickey Mouse in from 1928 to 1978?

Read the passage carefully to find out more about Mickey Mouse.

[1] Mickey Mouse celebrated his 50th birthday in 1978, and there were special events all over the country. There was even a party at the White House.

[2] Walt Disney and his partner Ub Iwerks created Mickey in 1928. At first, Mickey looked a little like Oswald the Rabbit, an old Disney character. This funny-looking little mouse was called Mortimer. Disney's wife didn't like the name, and her friends didn't either, so Disney changed it to Mickey. After 1938, Mickey's looks changed too.

[3] Mickey's first film, called "Plane Crazy," celebrated the transatlantic flight of Charles Lindbergh. It was a silent film like all cartoons made at that time. Later in 1928, Disney made "Steamboat Willie." This was the first animated cartoon with sound. The Colony Theater on Broadway in New York City showed the film, and Mickey became America's favorite cartoon star almost overnight.

[4] By 1929, Mickey Mouse was as popular as Coca-Cola. Mickey Mouse clubs started up all over the United States. By 1931, the Mickey Mouse Club had a million members. Mickey Mouse was popular all over the world. Italians called him Topolino. In London, Madame Tussaud's Wax Museum made Mickey in wax. From the White House in Washington, Eleanor Roosevelt wrote a letter to Walt Disney. She told him that President Roosevelt loved Mickey Mouse: "We . . . are all most grateful to you for many delightful evenings."

[5] Mickey was in more than 140 films from 1928 to 1978. There were also Mickey Mouse watches, toys, notebooks, etc. Today, many of the early Mickey Mouse items are very valuable.

[6] Mickey helped Walt Disney become a world-famous cartoonist. Young cartoonists went west to work with Disney, and he built his small cartoon business into a giant corporation. The Disney corporation made the first animated cartoon with sound and the first color cartoon. Mickey Mouse was the star in both.

[7] Some people say Walt Disney and Mickey were a lot alike. Both had nervous, high voices. Both liked adventure, both wanted to succeed, and both were true to their sweethearts.

35

[8] Why do people all over the world, young and old, like Mickey Mouse? Maybe it is just because he is a nice guy.

COMPREHENSION CHECK

General Questions

Mark the following statements TRUE or FALSE. Correct the false statements. Don't look back at the passage.

1. __T__   Mickey Mouse is now 50 years old.

2. __T__   Walt Disney and Ub Iwerks created Mickey Mouse.

3. __T__   Mickey's original name was Mortimer.

4. __T__   Mickey's first film was "Plane Crazy."

5. __F__   Mickey Mouse was not popular until 1978.

Factual Questions

Answer the following questions. You may look back at the passage.

1. How old was Mickey Mouse in 1978? How old is he this year?
2. What was the name of the first animated cartoon with sound?
3. How many members were in the Mickey Mouse Club in 1931?
4. What do the Italians call Mickey Mouse?
5. How many cartoon films did Mickey make in his first 50 years?
6. Who went west to work with Walt Disney?
7. What happened to Disney's small business?
8. How were Disney and Mickey Mouse alike?
9. Why do people probably like Mickey?

** Inferential Questions

Answer these questions. Read the passage again if necessary.

1. How did people celebrate Mickey's 50th birthday?
2. What did President Roosevelt think of Mickey Mouse?
3. Why did cartoonists go west to work with Disney?

What Do You Think?

1. Why do you think Mickey Mouse is so popular?
2. Are Mickey Mouse or other Walt Disney characters popular in your home country?
3. In your home country, do only children watch cartoons, or do adults enjoy them too?
4. What are some of your favorite cartoon characters? What kind of characters are they?

VOCABULARY SKILLS

Word Search

1. Write the word in line 4 that means *a teammate or person in business with you.*

   party

2. Write the word in line 6 that means *a person or animal in a book, film, etc.*

   _____

3. Write the word in line 13 to describe *a cartoon with lifelike movements.*

   animate

4. Write the word in line 20 that means *what candles are made of.*

   wax

5. Write the word in line 23 that means *thankful.*

   grateful

6. Write the word in line 23 that means *giving people joy and pleasure.*

   delightful

7. Write the word in line 27 that means *worth a lot of money.*

   _____

8. Write the word in line 34 that means the opposite of *relaxed.*

   _____

9. Write the word in line 34 that means *filled with excitement or danger.*

   _____

10. Write the word in line 35 that is similar to *darling.*

    _____

Word Families   Some words in English are used for men or women. Other words are used only for women or only for men. Look at this chart:

	Male Only	*Female Only*	*Male or Female*
1.	actor	actress	—
2.	—	—	partner
3.	—	—	character
4.	_____	gal	—
5.	_____	_____	_____
6.	_____	_____	_____
7.	_____	_____	_____
8.	_____	_____	_____
9.	_____	_____	_____
10.	_____	_____	_____
11.	_____	_____	_____
12.	_____	_____	_____
13.	_____	_____	_____
14.	_____	_____	_____
15.	_____	_____	_____

Write the following words in the correct place on the chart:

guy	player	boy	girl
husband	feminine	woman	adult
masculine	man	mother	father
child	uncle	parent	businessman
aunt	brother	businesswoman	
sister	wife	spouse	
businessperson	farmer	teacher	

Verbs → Nouns We can make verbs into nouns by adding the suffix *-er*. Finish writing the words on this list. Then complete the sentences on the right with the appropriate form.

	Verbs	*Nouns*	
1.	farm	farmer	A _____ usually works hard.
2.	_____	teacher	Some farmers _____ school part-time.
3.	camp	_____	I don't like to _____ .
4.	_____	player	He doesn't _____ tennis.
5.	sit	_____	He doesn't like children, so he won't make a good _____ .
6.	dance	_____	She likes to _____ .
7.	_____	singer	I have a terrible voice, so it is better if I don't _____ .
8.	build	_____	She helps _____ bridges.
9.	_____	designer	Clark is a dress _____ and lives in Manhattan.

10. work   _____   Lenin said,

"_____ of the

world, unite!"

11. help   _____   Can you _____

me with the homework?

READING SKILLS

Sentence Splitting   Look at this example:

> Disney's wife didn't like the name Mortimer, and her friends didn't either.

This sentence contains two sentences:

1. Disney's wife didn't like the name Mortimer.
2. Her friends didn't like the name Mortimer.

Split the following sentences:

A. John doesn't know how to use a computer, and Chris doesn't either.

     1. _____

     2. _____

B. Mr. Furleigh doesn't buy strawberries, and his wife doesn't either.

     1. _____

     2. _____

C. Cars aren't allowed on the parade route, and buses aren't either.

     1. _____

     2. _____

D. Abe Saperstein didn't make enough money, and his team didn't either.

     1. _____

     2. _____

E. Arabic isn't an easy language to learn, and Chinese isn't either.

1. _____

2. _____

Connections Connect the underlined word or group of words on the following page to the idea they refer to. Refer to the example on page 85 if necessary.

1. This strange little mouse was called Mortimer. Disney's wife didn't like <u>the name,</u> so Disney changed it to Mickey.

2. Later in the year, Disney made "Steamboat Willie," <u>the first animated cartoon with sound.</u>

3. The Colony Theater on Broadway showed the film, and Mickey became <u>America's favorite cartoon hero.</u>

4. Mickey Mouse was popular all over the world. Italians called him <u>Topolino.</u>

5. Mickey helped Walt Disney become <u>a world-famous cartoonist.</u>

6. The Disney corporation made the first animated cartoon with sound and the first color cartoon. Mickey Mouse was the star in <u>both.</u>

7. Some people say Walt Disney and Mickey were a lot alike. <u>Both</u> had nervous, high voices.

Main Ideas Choose the main idea. The main idea of

1. paragraph 1 is:
   a. Mickey had a 50th birthday.
   b. There were special events.
   c. There was a White House party for Mickey.

2. paragraph 2 is:
   a. Mickey was created.
   b. Walt Disney created cartoon characters.
   c. Oswald the Rabbit is a relative of Mickey Mouse.

3. paragraph 4 is:
   a. Mickey Mouse and Coca-Cola are connected.
   b. Mickey gained world-wide popularity.
   c. President Roosevelt loved Mickey Mouse.

4. paragraph 6 is:
   a. Mickey helped Disney become famous.
   b. Cartoonists went west.
   c. The Disney corporation made the first animated cartoon.

5. the whole passage is:
   a. After more than 50 years, Mickey is still popular all over the world.
   b. Mickey and Disney were a lot alike.
   c. Mickey was in more than 140 films.

READING 2

Read the passage carefully to find the answer to this question:

What was Walt Disney like?

Walt Disney: The Man Behind the Mouse

Walt Disney died in 1966, but his work and his dreams did not die. 1
A new generation of children watched his animated movies such as
"Snow White" and even his old Mickey Mouse cartoons. These are
the same Disney creations the parents and grandparents of these
children enjoyed. Millions of people also came to the United States 5
to enjoy Disneyland in California and Disney World and EPCOT in
Florida. But although Disney's work was extraordinary, in many
ways Walt Disney was an ordinary man. He was born in Chicago and
had a rather typical childhood in the Midwest. His family was not rich
or successful. In fact, his father failed in business several times. Walt 10
had to work hard, but he did not mind.

He did not mind hard work, and he did not give up easily. One
summer, Walt wanted a job at the post office, but they told him he
was too young. He went home, drew some lines on his face, and put
on his father's suit and hat. Then he went back to the same office and 15
told them he was 18. They gave him the job.

Later in his life, Disney had a dream. He wanted to build a new kind of amusement park. It would be clean and beautiful. There would be rides for children and nice restaurants for adults. It would be fun for people of all ages. Disney drew a plan for this park. It 20 was called Disneyland. Engineers told him it was an impossible dream. His family and friends told him it was crazy, but Disney did not give up his idea. In 1955, Disneyland opened its gates to the public and became the most successful amusement park in the United States. 25

COMPREHENSION CHECK

Answer these questions. You may look back at the passage.

1. What happened with Disney's work after he died?
2. What was ordinary about Disney's early life?
3. How did Disney feel about hard work?
4. Why didn't he get the post office job at first?
5. What helped him get the job?
6. What was Disney's dream in his later life?

VOCABULARY SKILLS

Idioms and Expressions   *to mind*

Look at this example from the passage:

Disney had to work hard, but he *did not mind.* (This means Disney did not dislike the hard work.)
Now look at this example:

MARILYN: *Would you mind* getting me a cup of coffee?

JOE: No, not at all. (I *don't mind* getting you coffee.) Would you like it with cream and sugar?

Now make questions using this idiom in the following situations. Ask someone to:

1. get you a cup of tea
2. help you with your homework
3. wash the car
4. give you a haircut
5. get off your foot

to give up

Look at these examples from the passage:

> 1. He did not mind hard work, and he did not *give up* easily.

(This means Disney did not stop trying to do something. He did not quit.)

> 2. Mary decided cigarettes were bad for her health, so she *gave up* smoking.

(This means Mary stopped smoking.)

Now answer these questions using the appropriate form of the idiom:

1. What do some people do when something is very difficult?

   _____

2. What do some people do when they find that studying English is difficult?

   _____

3. My son wants to go to France this summer, but he spends all his money on beer. What should I tell him to give up?

   _____

4. John is too fat. He eats lots of cake. What should he give up to become thin?

   _____

5. What do some people do when they want to save money?

   _____

Word Families   success (noun)   Mickey Mouse became an overnight *success.*

succeed (verb)   Disney wanted to *succeed.*
  succeeded
  succeeding
successful (adjective)   Disney became a *successful* cartoonist.
successfully (adverb)   He *successfully* made the first color cartoon.

Use the listed words to fill in the blanks:

Walt Disney's father was not a _____ businessman. In fact, his business failed several times. He wanted to _____, so he moved with his family several times to new towns. Each time he hoped for _____. Unfortunately, he did not find it.

life (noun)   His *life* was exciting.
living (noun)   *Living* was an adventure for him.
live (verb)   Disney *lived* in Hollywood.
  lived
  living
lively (adjective) Mickey is a *lively* mouse.

Use the listed words to fill in the blanks:

Disney _____ an ordinary _____ during his childhood. Later, he worked as a cartoonist for a few years. During this time, he drew _____ little cartoon characters.

READING SKILLS

Guessing Meanings from Context   Choose the best meaning for each italicized word. Use the context to help you.

1. A new *generation* of children watched his animated movies, such as "Snow White," and even his old Mickey Mouse cartoons. These are the same Disney creations the parents and grandparents of these children enjoyed.
   a. all people born about the same time
   b. a group of people
   c. students

2. But although Disney's work was *extraordinary,* in many ways Disney was an ordinary man. He was born in Chicago and had a rather typical childhood in the Midwest.
   a. expensive
   b. not typical or usual
   c. well-known

3. His family was not rich or successful. In fact, his father *failed* in business several times. Walt had to work hard, but he did not mind.
   a. learned a lot about something
   b. made a lot of money
   c. did not succeed

4. He wanted to build a new kind of *amusement park.* It would be clean and beautiful. There would be rides for children and nice restaurants for adults. It would be fun for all ages.
   a. place to enjoy oneself
   b. garden
   c. place to eat

5. Engineers told him it was *impossible.* His family and friends told him it was crazy, but Disney did not give up his idea.
   a. expensive
   b. not possible to do
   c. too much trouble

Pronoun Reference Draw an arrow connecting the circled words to the words they refer to.

Walt Disney and Ub Iwerks had an idea. (They) created a new cartoon character. (His) name was Mortimer. Disney's wife liked the little mouse, but (she) didn't like (his) name, so (they) decided to name (him) Mickey.

CHAPTER REVIEW Tell the story of Mickey Mouse in your own words.

_____

_____

_____

_____

POST-READING ACTIVITIES

Strip Story Put these events in logical order:

__ Ub Iwerks and Walt Disney created Mickey.

__ Mickey celebrated his 50th birthday.

__ The Mickey Mouse Club had 1 million members.

__ Mickey became as popular as Coca-Cola.

__ Mickey played in "Steamboat Willie."

__ Mickey played in "Plane Crazy."

__ Mickey's looks changed.

Word Pyramids Use the clues on the left to build the pyramids:

1. the 15th letter

2. not yes, but _____

3. He is _____ here.

4. a short letter

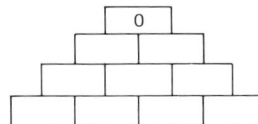

1. me

2. not out, but _____

3. your pen has this

4. a pretty color

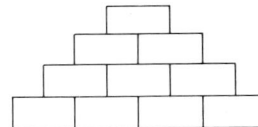

1. the 15th letter

2. not off, but _____

3. the male child

4. in the near future

5. you eat soup with this

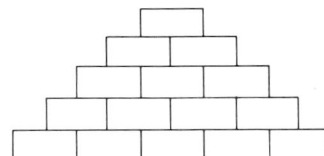

1. the 1st letter

2. _____ orange

3. in addition to

4. it has five fingers

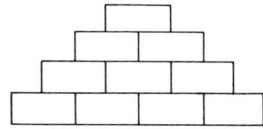

Up, Up, and Away!

PRE-READING

What are the objects in the picture?

What is the connection between the picture and the title?

READING 1

Balloon

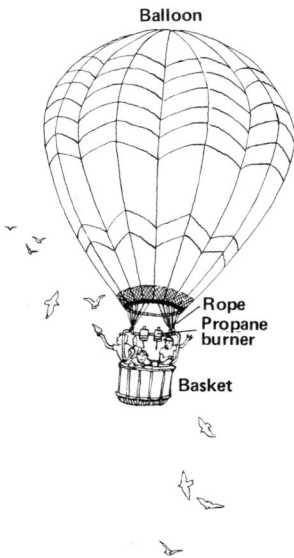

Rope
Propane
burner

Basket

Given Name	Nicknames
MALE	
William	Bill, Will, Billy
James	Jim, Jimmy
John	Jack, Johnny
FEMALE	
Susan	Sue, Susie
Barbara	Barb, Barbie
Katherine	Kate, Kathy

Scan the passage to find the answers to these questions:

1. Who is William Woodman?
2. How many hot-air balloons were in the United States in 1963?

Now read the passage carefully to learn the answer to this question:

Is ballooning dangerous?

1 The houses and cars below us look smaller and smaller. Over us, a giant, colorful balloon° carries our little basket° silently up to the sky. Every few minutes the pilot pulls the handle on one of the propane burners° and sends hot air into the balloon. This makes a loud sound: WHOOSH. We pass over neighborhood rooftops and over fields and small lakes. We watch farmers working, children playing, and horses and cows eating grass.

2 We are in a hot-air balloon. The pilot is Dr. William Woodman, or Bill to his friends. From Monday to Friday, he is a sociology professor at Iowa State University, but on weekends he is a hot-air balloon pilot. Many of Bill Woodman's friends want to go up in his balloon. Other people tell him, "Bill, you're crazy!" These people think ballooning is an unusual and dangerous hobby for a middle-aged, midwestern professor.

3 But hot-air ballooning is one of the fastest-growing sports in the United States. In 1963, there were only 6 hot-air balloons in the United States. Today, there are thousands. In fact, there are more hot-air balloons in the United States than in all the rest of the world.

4 Ballooning looks dangerous, but most hot-air balloonists say it is safer than driving a car. Landing is the biggest problem. In a strong wind, a pilot may have to bring the balloon down in trees or water. In the countryside, electric lines are a big problem for balloonists. Running into electric lines can be dangerous. New pilots learn how to avoid problems like these during many hours of instruction with an experienced pilot. At the end of this instruction, the new pilot receives a license.

5 I feel less nervous now. From the farmyard below, children look up and wave "hello," and we wave back. Dogs bark and horses run away. We see some cows. Bill uses propane to lift us higher. WHOOSH! He does not want to frighten them. Balloonists need

friendly farmers because open farmland is the best place to land a balloon.

⁶ Bill sees a green, grassy field near a farmhouse. He pulls a rope° to let air out of the balloon. We begin to drop slowly to the ground. "Hold on and try to relax," Bill tells me. Our basket lands. THUMP! ₃₅ Three friends run up and hold the ropes as we crawl out of the basket. Someone opens a bottle of champagne and pours a glass of it for each of us. Before we drink, I lift my glass and say, "To the pilot." Bill lifts his glass and says, "To ballooning."

COMPREHENSION CHECK

General Questions   Mark these statements TRUE or FALSE. Correct the false statements. Don't look back at the passage.

1. ___T___ The passage takes place in a hot-air balloon.

2. ___F___ There are fewer balloons today than ten years ago.

3. ___F___ Ballooning is very dangerous.

4. ___T___ A strong wind can cause problems for balloonists.

5. ___T___ Balloonists need friendly farmers.

6. ___T___ At the end of the balloon trip, there is champagne.

Factual Questions   Answer these questions. Read the passage again if necessary.

1. What happens when the pilot pulls the handle on the propane burner?
2. What do the people in the balloon see below?
3. What is the pilot's name?
4. What does the pilot do from Monday to Friday? What does he do on weekends?
5. What do some people say to the pilot?
6. How old is the pilot?
7. How many hot-air balloons were there in 1963?
8. How many hot-air balloons are there in the United States now?
9. What is the biggest problem in hot-air ballooning?

10. What does the pilot receive at the end of his instruction?
11. Where does Bill decide to land?
12. How does Bill let air out of the balloon?
13. What happens when Bill pulls the rope?
14. What do they do after they land?

✱✱ Inferential Questions   Answer these questions. Read the passage again if necessary.

1. Why do the houses and cars look smaller and smaller?
2. Why do dogs bark and horses run away when the balloon floats over them?
3. When does Bill pull a rope to let air out of the balloon?

What Do You Think?   1. Do you think ballooning is a crazy hobby for a middle-aged professor? Why or why not?
2. Are you surprised that ballooning is more popular in the United States than anywhere else? Why or why not?
3. What makes the United States a good place for ballooning?
4. Would you like to take a ride in a hot-air balloon? Why or why not?

VOCABULARY SKILLS

Word Search   1. Write the word in line 2 that means *with lots of color.*

_____

2. Write the word in line 2 that means *without noise.*

_____

3. Write the word in line 4 that means *a kind of gas.*

_____

4. Write the word in line 9 that means *the study of human society.*

_____

5. Write the word in line 13 that means *something you do for fun when you are not working.*

_____

6. Write the word in line 13 that means *in the middle of life.*

_____

7. Write the word in line 20 that means *coming down on the earth from the air.*

_____

8. Write the word in line 24 that means *to stay away from.*

_____

9. Write the word in line 26 that means *a piece of paper that gives you permission to do something, such as drive a car.*

_____

10. Write the word in line 29 that means *to move upward.*

_____

Opposites   Fill in the blanks with the appropriate word:

(lift/drop) (lower/higher)	The pilot pulls the handle and uses propane gas to _____ our balloon upward. We move _____.
(experienced/inexperienced)	Luckily, he knows a lot about ballooning, so he is not an _____ balloonist. His in-
(safe/dangerous)	structor is an excellent teacher, so our trip should be _____
(safe/dangerous)	unless something strange or _____ happens.

Compound Words   Many words in English contain two words. Sometimes a hyphen (-) connects them. A dictionary can help you decide if a word needs a hyphen.

Examples

baby + sit = baby-sit
some + one = someone

Complete the following compound words used in the passage:

1. hot-_____

2. farm_____

3. _____land

4. _____house

5. _____side

6. middle-_____

7. roof_____

READING SKILLS

Guessing Meanings from Context   Choose the best meaning for each italicized word. Use the context to help you.

1. From Monday to Friday he is a sociology professor at Iowa State University, but on *weekends* he is a hot-air balloon pilot.
   a. Monday to Friday
   b. Saturday and Sunday
   c. holidays

2. Ballooning looks *dangerous,* but most hot-air balloonists say it is safer than driving a car.
   a. not safe
   b. safe
   c. difficult

3. Dogs bark and horses run away. We see some cows. Bill uses propane to lift us higher. WHOOSH! He does not want to *frighten* them. Balloonists need friendly farmers because open farmland is the best place to land a balloon.
   a. make . . . afraid
   b. make . . . sick
   c. make . . . dangerous

4. Running into electric lines can be dangerous. New pilots learn how to *avoid* problems like these during many hours with an experienced pilot.
   a. stay away from
   b. take care of
   c. do

5. He pulls a rope to let air out of the balloon. We begin to *drop* slowly to the ground.
   a. pass
   b. fall
   c. fly

Pronoun Reference Draw arrows connecting the circled words to the words they refer to.

We are in a hot-air balloon. (It) is passing over the countryside below. The pilot is Dr. William Woodman. (He) is a sociology professor at Iowa State University and a hot-air balloonist. Many of his friends say (they) want to go up in his balloon. Other people tell (him) that it is a crazy idea.

Bill and I see a grassy field. (It) looks like a good place to land. After (we) land, three friends run up to us. (They) take the ropes and hold (them) as we crawl out of the basket.

Main Ideas Choose the main idea. The main idea of

1. paragraph 2 is:
   a. Professor Woodman is a sociology professor and hot-air balloon pilot.
   b. Middle-aged professors can be hot-air balloon pilots.
   c. Ballooning is too dangerous for a middle-aged professor.

2. paragraph 3 is
   a. Ballooning is a fast-growing sport in the United States.
   b. Ballooning is a hobby for thousands of people.
   c. Ballooning is a sport.

3. paragraph 4 is:
   a. Ballooning has its dangers.
   b. There are licenses for balloonists.
   c. Strong winds are a problem for balloonists.

4. the whole passage is:
   a. Some people think Bill Woodman is crazy.
   b. Ballooning is dangerous.
   c. Ballooning is a fun and fast-growing sport.

READING 2   Read the passage to find out why its title is appropriate.

Flying Father and Son

Maxie Anderson and his 23-year-old son Kris flew from California 1
to Quebec. It was a 3100-mile (4988 km) trip, and it took 100 hours.
But this was no ordinary flight. There were no passengers. Maxie and
Kris were alone. There was not even a plane. The pilot and co-pilot
were in a balloon.   5

Maxie and Kris wanted to make the first nonstop balloon trip
across North America. They started in San Francisco, California, and
hoped to land in Kitty Hawk, North Carolina. But the Andersons had
some bad luck. Strong winds blew them 1100 miles (1770 km) north,
and they landed near the forests of Quebec. There were other prob-   10
lems on the trip too. Flying over the Rocky Mountains was cold.
There was also little air, so they needed to take oxygen.

After the trip, Kris said he did not want any more adventures.
"Once was enough," he said. But his 43-year-old father did not agree,
"Man always has a dream. I'm sure I'll think of something else to try." 15

Adapted from *People*

**COMPREHENSION
CHECK**

Answer these questions. You may look back at the passage.

1. What did Maxie Anderson and his son do?
2. Where did they start their trip?
3. Where did they want to land?
4. Why did they land in Quebec?
5. What problems did they have on their trip?
6. After their trip, did Kris want to have another adventure with his
   father? Why or why not?
7. Did Maxie Anderson want to make another trip?

VOCABULARY SKILLS

Idioms and Expressions   even

Even **is often used for emphasis.**

Examples

1. I was in a hurry and had no time to pack my things. There wasn't *even* time to get my toothbrush.

2. He was hungry and thirsty, but they gave him nothing to eat or drink. They didn't *even* give him a glass of water.

3. She makes a lot of money. She *even* drives a Mercedes

Complete the following sentences:

1. I am very poor. I don't even

_____.

2. That man is very rich. He even has

_____.

3. That computer does almost everything. It even

_____.

Affixes   The prefix *non-* means "no" or "not."

Examples

1. Maxie and Kris wanted to make the first *non*stop balloon trip across the United States = They wanted to cross the United States without stopping.

2. He will lose his car for *non*payment. = He will lose his car because he did not make payments on it.

Read the following sentences. Use the context to help you decide the meaning of the italicized word. Then write the meaning in the space provided.

1. Don't offer her a cigarette. She is a *nonsmoker*.

_____

2. He wants to join the club, but he is still a *nonmember*.

_____

3. You are crazy, and you are talking *nonsense*.

_____

4. Some people like to read fiction, but I don't. I like to read about things that really happened, so I read *nonfiction*.

_____

Word Families flight (noun) Our *flight* was late.
flying (noun) I like *flying*.
fly (verb) I *fly* to Denver every spring.
  flew
  flying

Use the listed words to fill in the blanks:

I want to _____ home for the holidays. I need a _____ that leaves on December 15th. _____ at that time of year is usually difficult. Last year, I _____ to New York, but there was a delay in Chicago, so our _____ was late.

balloon (noun)	Children usually like *balloons*.
ballooning (noun)	*Ballooning* is fun, even for adults.
balloonist (noun-person)	*Balloonists* practice flying with experienced pilots.

dream (noun)	His *dream* is to be a balloonist.
dreaming (noun)	*Dreaming* is enjoyable.
dreamer (noun-person)	He is a *dreamer*, but does little work.
dream (verb)	Everyone *dreams* while sleeping.
dreamed	
dreaming	

Use the listed words to fill in the blanks:

_____ is great fun. Would you like to be a _____? The first thing you'll need is a _____. But _____ are usually expensive.

    Still, you can _____. Sometimes _____ is good for you. And some _____ become balloonists.

electricity (noun)	When did *electricity* come to the village?
electrician (noun-person)	*Electricians* set up and repair electrical systems.
electric (adjective)	There are no *electric* lights in our house on the lake.

Use the listed words to fill in the blanks:

This morning when I turned on the water, it was cold instead of hot. Then I turned on my _____ coffee maker, but nothing happened. There was no _____. I called an _____. She told me to look out my window. The _____ lines were down.

READING SKILLS

Pronoun Reference Draw arrows connecting the circled words to the words they refer to.

Maxie Anderson and his son took a trip in a balloon. (They) started in California. After (their) trip, Kris said (he) didn't want any more adventures, but his father said, "(I'm) sure I'll think of something else to try."

CHAPTER REVIEW

1. Describe a hot-air balloon.

_____

_____

_____

2. List three possible dangers of hot-air ballooning.

_____

_____ _____

_____

POST-READING ACTIVITIES

Strip Story Number these events in logical order:

_____ Kris says he does not want any more adventures.

_____ Maxie and Kris leave California.

_____ Maxie and Kris decide to cross the United States in a balloon.

_____ They fly over the Rocky Mountains.

_____ They buy a balloon for the trip.

_____ They land near Quebec.

_____ Mrs. Anderson kisses her son and husband good-bye.

Word Search Puzzle Names of people in the passages from Chapters 1 to 9 follow. This list of names has only the first names. Find the last names in the passages and then in the word puzzle. The names can go forward, backward, up, down, or diagonally.

Maxie _____	A H G I E L R U F N
Denison _____	B O L L A Y A X I E
John _____	E (R O O S E V E L T)
Walt _____	C O R K E N T U B E
Bob _____	A N D E R S O N Y S
Ub _____	P E A O R I S O N U
Charles _____	H G R E B D N I L O
Mickey _____	A R P D R A N O B M
Eleanor *Roosevelt*	N A M D O O W A L T
Abe _____	S K R E W I C K E Y
Bill _____	

**A Balloon Trip over
Iowa State University**

Bill Woodman is flying his balloon over the Iowa State University campus. He points out the sights below to his passenger. Look at the map and fill in the names of the places they see.

Look! You can see the campus over there. There's the graduate dormitory and across the street is the *president's house*. That very large building west of his home is the Memorial union. As we're going west, we cross Morrill Road and go over Lake laverne . Look, you can see the ducks swimming on it. The wind is moving us north toward central campus. As we pass over the sidewalk on central campus, on our right is CURTISS Hall and on our left is Central . North of central campus is _____, the oldest building on campus. That large building to the west of it is the

_____.

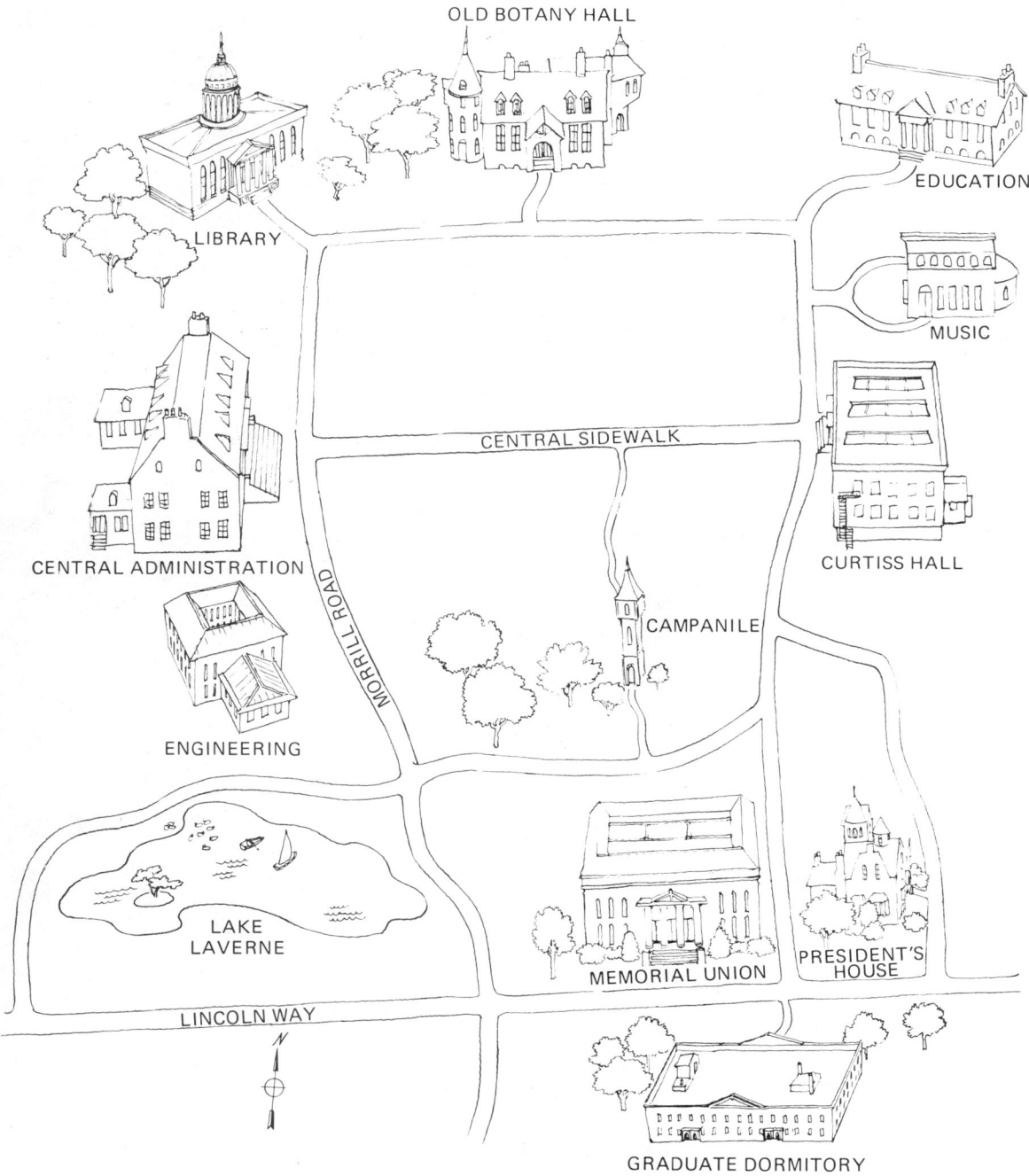

OLD BOTANY HALL

LIBRARY

EDUCATION

MUSIC

CENTRAL SIDEWALK

CURTISS HALL

CENTRAL ADMINISTRATION

MORRILL ROAD

CAMPANILE

ENGINEERING

LAKE LAVERNE

MEMORIAL UNION

PRESIDENT'S HOUSE

LINCOLN WAY

N

GRADUATE DORMITORY

Nobody Can Do It Like McDonald's

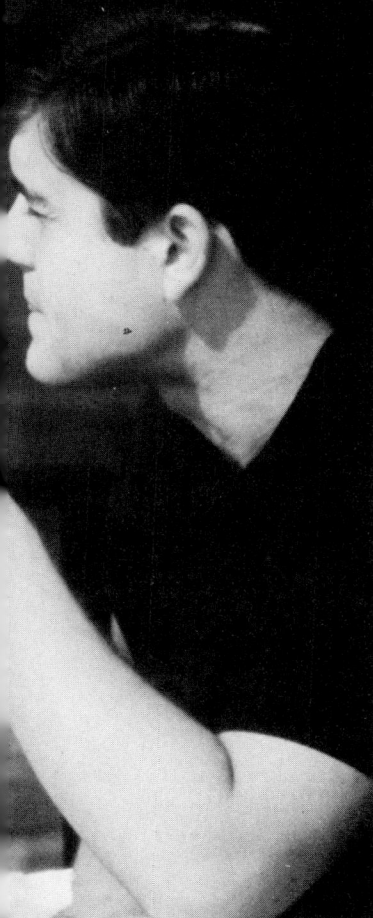

PRE-READING
Look at the picture.
Where are the people?
What are they doing?

READING 1

Scan the passage to find the answers to these questions:

1. Who is the past president of McDonald's?
2. When did the McDonald brothers open their first restaurant?
3. How much did Ray Kroc pay for the McDonald brothers' restaurants?

Now read the passage carefully to learn the answers to this question:

Why is McDonald's popular?

¹ Fast-food restaurants are very popular in the United States. They   1
are popular because the service is fast and the prices are low. Of all
the fast-food restaurants, McDonald's is probably the most famous
and the most popular.

² McDonald's is popular for several reasons. Customers can get the   5
same food at any McDonald's in any state or country. The employees
are helpful and polite, and the tables and floors are clean. Ray Kroc,
past president of McDonald's, believed that helpful employees, a
clean restaurant, and good food were necessary.

³ And McDonald's customers *do* like the food. They like the sand-   10
wiches, the milk shakes, and the French fries. Of all the items on
McDonald's menu, the French fries are probably the most popular.
They are good because of their special preparation.

⁴ Richard and Maurice McDonald, the original owners of McDonald's, had their own special preparation of French fries. In 1948, they   15
opened their first self-service restaurant in San Bernardino, California. People would come from everywhere to buy their French fries
and hamburgers. Workers would buy their lunches at McDonald's
because the hamburgers and French fries tasted better than their
lunches from home.   20

⁵ By 1960, the McDonald brothers owned 228 self-service restaurants. Then, in 1960, Ray Kroc, a 56-year-old salesman, bought the
name and most of the restaurants for $2.7 million.

⁶ He then began to build new restaurants, and, by 1982, he owned
about 7063. Of those restaurants, about 1283 were in other countries: 25
Japan, West Germany, England, and Australia. That same year, Mc-
Donald's Corporation earned about $7 billion.

⁷ McDonald's is a big business, but it is not too big or too rich to
help ordinary people. For example, owners of restaurants participate

Ronald McDonald®

in special community programs for children or senior citizens. Other　30
owners have carnivals to get money for medical research.

⁸ The corporation owns special houses near children's hospitals.
These Ronald McDonald° houses are for sick children and their parents. Sometimes a child has to stay at a hospital for several weeks or
months. Then the child's parents can stay at a Ronald McDonald　35
house. Staying at these houses is cheaper than staying at hotels, and
the atmosphere is friendlier and more <u>homelike.</u>

⁹ People don't go to McDonald's because of community programs
or Ronald McDonald houses. They go because of the food, the fast
service, and the low prices. They are like David Green. He says,　40
"McDonald's is my favorite place to eat in the whole world. I
wouldn't move to any town that didn't have one."

COMPREHENSION CHECK

General Questions　Look at the statements that follow. Correct them if necessary and
add other ideas from the passage. Follow these examples:

STATEMENT:　McDonald's is a popular fast-food restaurant.

STUDENT 1:　Yes. McDonald's is one of the most popular fast-food restaurants.

STUDENT 2:　McDonald's is one of the most famous fast-food restaurants.

STATEMENT:　The service at McDonald's is slow.

STUDENT 1:　No, the service is fast.

STUDENT 2:　The service is fast, and the prices are low.

1. People go to McDonald's because they like the food.
2. The first McDonald's was famous for its clean tables.
3. Richard McDonald bought the restaurants from Ray Kroc.
4. The McDonald's Corporation earned money in 1982.
5. Owners of McDonald's participate in community programs.
6. McDonald's special houses are only for sick employees.
7. Living at a Ronald McDonald house is cheaper than living at a
hotel.

Factual Questions   Answer these questions. You may look back at the passage.

1. Why are fast-food restaurants popular?
2. Who opened the first McDonald's restaurant? Where? When?
3. What kind of restaurant did they have?
4. When did Ray Kroc buy the restaurants from the McDonald brothers?
5. What other countries have McDonald's restaurants?
6. What kind of community programs do owners participate in?
7. Why do some owners have carnivals?
8. Why do parents stay at Ronald McDonald houses?

✱✱ Inferential Questions   Answer these questions. Read the passage again if necessary.

1. Why does Ray Kroc want good food, helpful employees, and clean floors and tables at his restaurants?
2. Why did Ray Kroc buy the name from the McDonald brothers?
3. What kind of food does David Green probably like?

What Do You Think?
1. Do you like to eat at McDonald's or other fast-food restaurants? Why or why not?
2. Is there a McDonald's in your city or country? If there is, is it popular? What kind of people go there?
3. Would you want McDonald's to build a restaurant in your city or country? If you do, would it be popular? Why or why not?
4. McDonald's owners work 50 or more hours a week, but they can earn $60,000 or $70,000 a year. Would you like to own a McDonald's? Why or why not?

VOCABULARY SKILLS

Word Search   1. Write the word in line 6 that means *people who work for other people.*

_____

2. Write the word in line 16 that means *serve yourself.*

_____

3. Write the word in line 30 that means *a group of people living in the same area.*

    —————————————

4. Write the words in line 30 that mean *people 65 years or older.*

    —————————————

5. Write the word in line 34 that means almost the same as *to be in a place.*

    —————————————

6. Write the word in line 37 that means *similar to home.*

    —————————————

Opposites   Fill in the blanks with the appropriate word:

(popular / unpopular)   1. Henry's Hamburger House is very —————————————. There are always a lot of people eating there.

(employed / unemployed)   2. When you are not working, you are —————————————.

(friendly / unfriendly)   3. Ann never talks to anyone. I think she's —————————————.

(helpful / unhelpful)   4. It is ————————————— but unnecessary to carry your dishes out to the kitchen.

(common / uncommon)   5. It is ————————————— for children in the United States to go to school on Saturday.

Affixes   We can change some nouns to adjectives by adding the suffix *-ful* at the end of the word: *-ful* means "full of."

> *Example*
>
> help (noun) → helpful (adjective)
> John cleaned the garage. He was very *helpful*.

Fill in the blanks with the appropriate word:

(hope/hopeful)   1. "There's no _____ for this car," the mechanic said. "It's too old."

2. I am _____ that I will pass the test.

3. "You shouldn't be too _____," said the doctor to the man's wife.

(help/helpful)   4. I need your _____ with the dishes.

5. "_____!" shouted the balloonist when he fell out of the basket.

6. A dictionary can be _____ sometimes.

(care/careful)   7. Bob takes good _____ of the children when he baby-sits.

8. "Be _____," says the police officer. "The parade is coming down the street."

9. Mary drives 25 miles an hour (40.2 km per hour) in the city. She's a very _____ driver.

(use/useful)   10. Do you have any _____ for an umbrella with holes?

11. An umbrella with holes is not

_____.

12. If you want to be _____, you can clean the tables.

Word Families ownership (noun)   Under Kroc's *ownership*, the company
                                       earned $3.1 billion.
                 owner (noun-person)   Ray Kroc is the *owner* of McDonald's.
                 own (verb)   Ray Kroc *owns* McDonald's.
                   owned
                   owning

Use the listed words to fill in the blanks:

Mr. Dasher always wanted to _____ a McDonald's restaurant. Ten years ago, he became the _____ of his first restaurant in Ames, Iowa. Now he _____ four restaurants. Under his _____, the restaurants are doing well and are earning him a lot of money.

employment (noun)   A high school student can find *employ-
                      ment* at McDonald's.
employee (noun-person) The *employees* at McDonald's are po-
                        lite.
employer (noun-person) Mr. Dasher is the *employer* of the work-
                        ers at his restaurants.
employ (verb)   McDonald's *employs* thousands of peo-
  employed   ple.
  employing

Use the listed words to fill in the blanks:

John needs money for school, so he is looking for some kind of _____. Mr. Dasher owns a self-service restaurant. He _____ many high school students. Some of John's friends are _____ there. John's friends like their work and Mr. Dasher, their _____. So, John went to the restaurant to talk to the owner about getting a job.

JOHN: I'm looking for some part-time _____. Do you have any openings?

OWNER: You're in luck! I need a full-time and a part-time _____ right now. Why don't you sit down and fill out this application?

READING SKILLS

Pronoun Reference   Draw arrows connecting the circled words to the words they refer to.

People go to McDonald's because of the food, the fast service, and the low prices. (They) are like David Green. (He) says, "(It's) my favorite place to eat in the whole world. (I) wouldn't move to any town that didn't have (one.)"

Main Ideas   Choose the main idea. The main idea of

1. paragraph 2 is:
   a. McDonald's is the most famous fast-food restaurant.
   b. McDonald's is popular for several reasons.
   c. The employees are helpful and polite.

2. paragraph 4 is:
   a. Richard and Maurice McDonald were the original owners.
   b. They opened their first restaurant in 1948.
   c. People liked the first McDonald's because of their hamburgers and French fries.

3. paragraph 7 is:
   a. McDonald's is big business.
   b. McDonald's helps ordinary people.
   c. Owners participate in community programs.

4. paragraph 8 is:
   a. McDonald's Corporation owns houses.
   b. Ronald McDonald helps sick children.
   c. McDonald's tries to help sick children and their parents.

READING 2 Read the passage to learn the answer to this question:

How do people become owners of McDonald's restaurants?

A Good Business

Because McDonald's is a good business, thousands of people apply   1
for restaurant ownership each year. McDonald's, however, chooses
only 10 percent of the applicants. Every year, many businesspeople,
doctors, or lawyers quit their jobs to become owners. Guy Roderick,
a lawyer, gave up his law practice, moved to Florida, and opened 4   5
restaurants. He works every day of the week, but he earns "a million
dollars in happiness."

It is not easy to become the owner of a McDonald's restaurant.
New applicants must first observe and then work in a McDonald's
restaurant for about 500 hours. Then they spend 10 days at Ham-   10
burger University. There they learn everything about owning a restaurant. They learn how to clean a grill, how much food to buy, and
how to balance the books. They graduate with a major in "hambur-
gerology" and a minor in "French fries."

The applicant's name then goes to the bottom of a list. When each   15
name gets to the top of the list, the applicant gets a restaurant.
Applicants cannot choose a city or town, but they can accept or reject
a location.

After the new owner accepts a location, he or she chooses the basic
design of the restaurant. Most McDonald's look almost the same on   20
the outside, but actually there are about 16 different basic designs.
Then the owner designs the inside of the restaurant. The design may
have a Western, a sports, or a historical theme. Each design, however, will suit each owner's taste.

**COMPREHENSION
CHECK** Answer the following questions. You may look back at the passage.

1. How many applicants does McDonald's choose?
2. What kind of people become owners of McDonald's restaurants?
3. What must new applicants do?
4. What university do applicants go to?

5. What do applicants major in at the university?
6. When does an applicant get a restaurant?
7. Can applicants choose their own locations?
8. Who designs a new restaurant?
9. Do all McDonald's restaurants look alike on the outside? On the inside? Why are they different?

VOCABULARY SKILLS

Affixes   You can change some adjectives to nouns by adding *-ness* or *-iness.*

Example:

Guy Roderick is *happy* now. (adjective)
He earns a million dollars in *happiness.* (noun)

Fill in the blanks with the appropriate word:

(kind/kindness)   1. Our neighbors are very _____ people.

(sad/sadness)   2. The child's face was full of _____.

(red/redness)   3. My jacket is _____. What color is yours?

(fresh/freshness)   4. After a rain, there is always a _____ smell in the air.

(useful/usefulness)   5. "Get out!" said the boss to his employee. "I bought this wonderful machine, and now your _____ is over."

(weak/weakness)   6. Mary has a _____ for chocolate.

Word Families

application (noun)	He went to the store and filled out an *application*.
applicant (noun-person)	Mr. Jones, the Personnel Manager, talks with all *applicants*.
apply (verb) applied applying	John wanted to *apply* for a job.

Use the listed words to fill in the blanks:

MRS. PAUL: Good morning. Are you an _____?

ROGER: Excuse me?

MRS. PAUL: Are you _____ for a job?

ROGER: Oh. Yes, I am.

MRS. PAUL: Good. Here's an _____ for you to fill out. Do you have a Social Security number?

ROGER: No, I don't.

MRS. PAUL: I'm sorry. You must _____ for a Social Security number first. Then bring us your _____. Mrs. Johnson sees all _____ on Thursday afternoons.

READING SKILLS

Sentence Splitting Look at this example:

The design may have a Western, a sports, or a historical theme.

The sentence contains three sentences:

1. The design may have a Western theme.
2. The design may have a sports theme.
3. The design may have a historical theme.

Split these sentences:

A. Guy Roderick gave up his law practice, moved to Florida, and opened four restaurants.

1. _____

2. _____

3. _____

B. They learn how to clean a grill, how much food to buy, and how to balance the books.

    1. _____

    2. _____

    3. _____

C. Every few minutes, the pilot pulls the handle on one of the propane burners and sends hot air into the balloon.

    1. _____

    2. _____

D. Walt went home, drew some lines on his face, and put on his father's suit.

    1. _____

    2. _____

    3. _____

E. The boys learn how to change diapers and what to do in emergencies.

    1. _____

    2. _____

Scanning

DRIVE · THRU SERVICE

CHICKEN McNUGGETS	1.25
McCHICKEN SANDWICH	1.20
BIG MAC	1.30
QUARTER POUNDER with cheese	1.30
QUARTER POUNDER	1.15
FILET -O- FISH	90
CHEESEBURGER	60
HAMBURGER	50
FRENCH FRIES	52 / 87
HOT PIE apple or cherry	.45
SHAKES chocolate vanilla strawberry	.70
SUNDAES hot fudge hot caramel strawberry	.50
McDONALDLAND COOKIES	35
CHOCOLATY CHIP COOKIES	.40

CAMP SNOOPY GLASSES ARE HERE! ONLY AT McDONALD'S

Just each plus tax, with purchase of a medium or large Coca-Cola or other soft drink at the usual price.

NEW diet Coke One Calorie McDonald's

COCA - COLA ROOTBEER	505565
ORANGE DIET 7 UP	5055A5
COFFEE	35
MILK	45
ICED TEA	.55
GIFT CERTIFICATE	.50
BREAKFAST 7-10:30 AM	
SCRAMBLED EGGS Sausage & Hash Browns	1.60
HOT CAKES & SAUSAGE	1.25
EGG McMUFFIN	.99
SCRAMBLED EGGS & ENGLISH MUFFIN	.79
HOT CAKES	.69
DANISH	.50
HASH BROWNS	.45
JUICE orange grapefruit tomato	.45
ENGLISH MUFFIN with jelly	.40

Look at McDonald's menu and answer these questions:

1. What can you order for breakfast?
2. What sandwiches are *not* made with hamburger?
3. What kinds of drinks does McDonald's sell?
4. What can you order for dessert?
5. How much would a Big Mac, large fries, and a medium orange cost?

CHAPTER REVIEW

1. Give some reasons for McDonald's popularity.

_____

_____

_____

_____

2. Give some information about the first McDonald's.

_____

_____

_____

_____

3. Explain how McDonald's helps people and communities.

_____

_____

_____

_____

4. Tell what a person must do to become the owner of a McDonald's.

_____

_____

_____

_____

POST-READING ACTIVITIES

You need to apply for a Social Security number. Fill out the application below.

DEPARTMENT OF HEALTH AND HUMAN SERVICES
SOCIAL SECURITY ADMINISTRATION

Form Approved
OMB No. 0960-0066

FORM SS-5 – APPLICATION FOR A
SOCIAL SECURITY NUMBER CARD
(Original, Replacement or Correction)

MICROFILM REF. NO. (SSA USE ONLY)

Unless the requested information is provided, we may not be able to issue a Social Security Number (20 CFR 422.103(b))

INSTRUCTIONS TO APPLICANT ▶ Before completing this form, please read the instructions on the opposite page. You can type or print, using pen with dark blue or black ink. Do not use pencil.

		First	Middle	Last
NAA	NAME TO BE SHOWN ON CARD			
NAB	FULL NAME AT BIRTH (IF OTHER THAN ABOVE)	First	Middle	Last
ONA	OTHER NAME(S) USED			

1

STT	MAILING ADDRESS	(Street/Apt. No., P.O. Box, Rural Route No.)		
CTY STE ZIP	CITY		STATE	ZIP CODE

2

CSP CITIZENSHIP (Check one only)

3
- ☐ a U.S. citizen
- ☐ b Legal alien allowed to work
- ☐ c Legal alien not allowed to work
- ☐ d Other (See instructions on Page 2)

SEX **4**
- ☐ Male
- ☐ Female

ETB **5** RACE/ETHNIC DESCRIPTION (Check one only) (Voluntary)
- ☐ a. Asian, Asian American or Pacific Islander (Includes persons of Chinese, Filipino, Japanese, Korean, Samoan, etc., ancestry or descent)
- ☐ b. Hispanic (Includes persons of Chicano, Cuban, Mexican or Mexican-American, Puerto Rican, South or Central American, or other Spanish ancestry or descent)
- ☐ c. Negro or Black (not Hispanic)
- ☐ d. North American Indian or Alaskan Native
- ☐ e. White (not Hispanic)

DOB **6**	DATE OF BIRTH	MONTH	DAY	YEAR	AGE **7**	PRESENT AGE	PLB **8**	PLACE OF BIRTH	CITY	STATE OR FOREIGN COUNTRY

MNA **9**	MOTHER'S NAME AT HER BIRTH	First	Middle	Last (her maiden name)
FNA	FATHER'S NAME	First	Middle	Last

PNO a. Have you or someone on your behalf applied for a social security number before? ☐ No ☐ Don't Know ☐ Yes

10 *If you checked "yes", complete items "b" through "e" below; otherwise go to item 11.*

SSN PNS PNY	b. Enter social security number	c. In what State did you apply?	What year?

NLC	d. Enter the name shown on your most recent social security card	e. If the birth date you used was different from the date shown in item 6, enter it here	MONTH	DAY	YEAR

DON **11**	TODAY'S DATE	MONTH	DAY	YEAR	**12**	Telephone number where we can reach you during the day	HOME	OTHER

ASO WARNING: **Deliberately providing false information on this application is punishable by a fine of $1,000 or one year in jail, or both.**

13 YOUR SIGNATURE

14 YOUR RELATIONSHIP TO PERSON IN ITEM 1 ☐ Self ☐ Other (Specify) _____

WITNESS (Needed only if signed by mark "X")

WITNESS (Needed only if signed by mark "X")

DO NOT WRITE BELOW THIS LINE (FOR SSA USE ONLY)		DTC	SSA RECEIPT DATE _____
☐ SUPPORTING DOCUMENT- EXPEDITE CASE ☐ DUP ISSUED	SSN ASSIGNED OR VERIFIED SSN	NPN	
DOC	NTC	CAN	BIC	SIGNATURE AND TITLE OF EMPLOYEE(S) REVIEWING EVIDENCE AND/OR CONDUCTING INTERVIEW

TYPE(S) OF EVIDENCE SUBMITTED

☐ MANDATORY IN PERSON INTERVIEW CONDUCTED

DATE

DATE

IDN ITV DCL

Form **SS-5** (10-81)

Word Search Puzzle   Find and circle the following words in the puzzle:

BIG MAC	KETCHUP
CHEESEBURGER	LETTUCE
CHICKEN MCNUGGETS™	MAYONNAISE
COOKIES	MILK SHAKES
DOUBLE CHEESEBURGER	MUSTARD
DRINKS	ONIONS
FILET-O-FISH™	PICKLES
FRENCH FRIES	QUARTER POUNDER
FRUIT PIES	SESAME SEED
HAMBURGER	SUNDAES

```
D R I N K S E C I G C E T F C B T R
T A F H N S L E T T U C E I N I E N
A D E R E G R U B M A H H I A G D C
N L R S U H A N U M U I T A R M E S
M I E K S I A S E S Q C O U A A E E
I L D A K S T A R D U K B Y O C S I
L P N H N A A P I E A E O R P W E R
K I U E R C S T I M S N Q U X A M F
S C O D N O I N O E N M H A T B A H
H L P O N O N Y E A S C O O R A S C
A K R U A K E H I P T N E N A M E N
K E E B I I C S R E S U N D A E S E
E C T L S E E C K A R G O R I N K R
S H R D L S T I R D Y G N I N O S F
O E A B O N A F F I L E T O F I S H
U E U R C B N I C F H T S N O I N O
N O Q U A P I C K L E S H K E S H I
D R I N R T R E G R U B E S E E H C
```

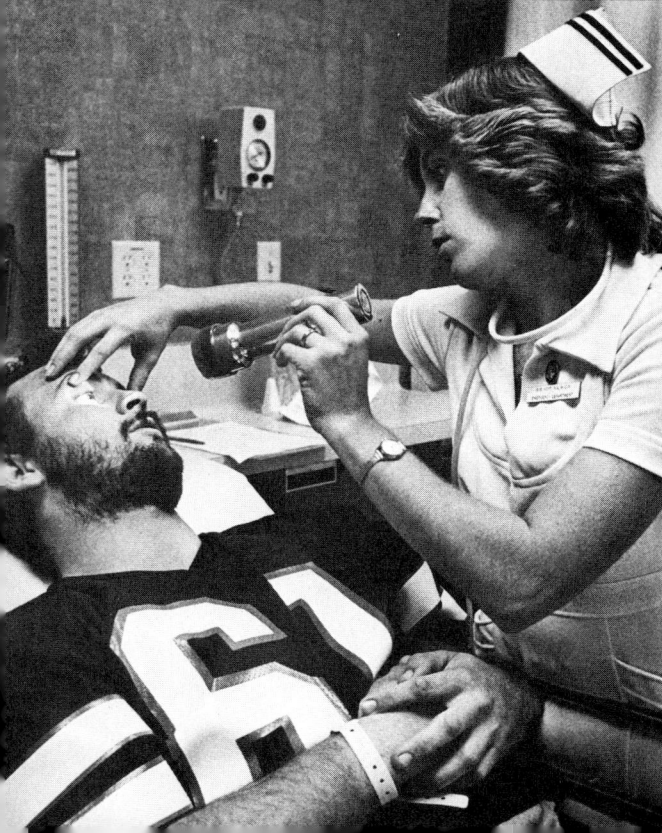
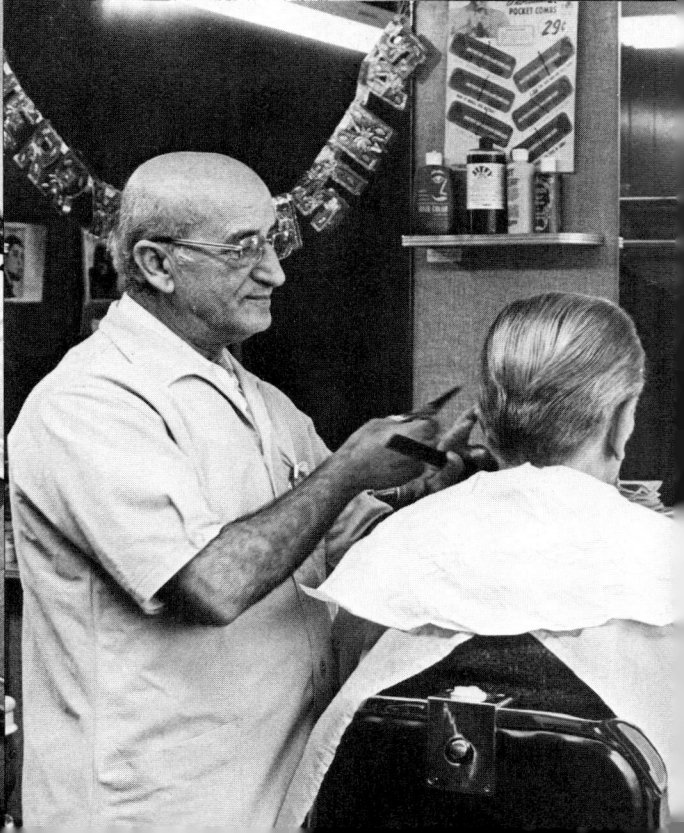

Adult Education

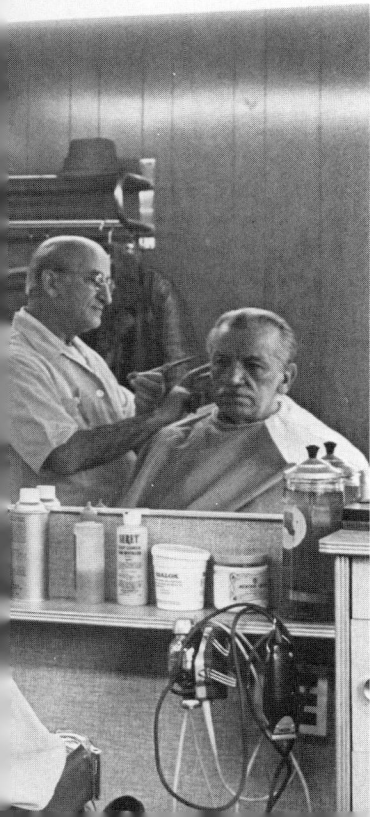

PRE-READING

Give the occupation of the person in each picture.

What skills do these people need? For example, a secretary must know how to type. Typing is a skill.

READING 1

Scan the passage to find the answers to these questions:

1. What language classes can people choose?
2. How many people register for adult classes each year?

Now read the passage carefully to learn the answer to this question:

Why do people take continuing education classes?

¹ Ideas about education are changing in the United States. Educa- 1
tion today is not just a high school diploma or a college degree. Many
adults are not interested in going to college. They are interested in
other kinds of learning. For them, learning does not end with a
diploma. 5

² Continuing education gives these adults the opportunity to increase their knowledge about their own field or to learn about a new
field. It also gives them a chance to improve their old skills or to learn
new ones.

³ Secretaries, mechanics, and barbers can take classes to improve 10
their work skills. Nurses can take classes to increase their knowledge
of nursing. If they know more or learn more, then they can get a
better job or earn more money.

⁴ Continuing education classes give some adults the chance to
learn new skills. There is usually a large variety of classes to choose 15
from: typing, foreign cooking, photography, auto repair, furniture
repair, or swimming. These are only some of the classes available.

⁵ Some adults take classes for fun or because the class will be useful
for them. For example, they can choose a class in almost any language: Arabic, Spanish, or English as a second language. There are 20
classes in first aid or classes in sewing. There are also many other
types of classes to choose from.

⁶ Other adults take continuing education classes to improve their
own lives because they want to feel better about themselves. Overweight people can find exercise classes or classes in nutrition. Others 25
can learn how to be good parents, or how to get along with other
people.

⁷ There are many opportunities for adults to continue their learning. Almost any community college or public school system has a
continuing education program. There are classes in schools, commu- 30
nity buildings, or churches. Most classes are in the evening, so work-

ing people can attend. The classes are usually small, and they are inexpensive.

[8] Thousands of people register for continuing education classes each year. They receive no diploma or certificate, and no grade for 35 most of the classes they attend. For them, learning is something they do because they want to.

COMPREHENSION CHECK

General Questions Look at the following statements: Correct them if necessary and add other ideas from the passage. Follow these examples:

> STATEMENT: Education is only a diploma.
>
> STUDENT 1: No. Education is not only a diploma.
>
> STUDENT 2: Education does not end with a diploma.

> STATEMENT: People can study almost any language.
>
> STUDENT 1: Yes. People can study almost any language.
>
> STUDENT 2: People can study Arabic, Spanish, or English as a second language.

1. Secretaries can take courses to improve their skills.
2. There are only a few classes to choose from.
3. Some people take classes to improve themselves.
4. There aren't many opportunities for adults to continue their learning.
5. Most continuing education classes meet during the day.

Factual Questions Answer these questions. You may look back at the passage.

1. Why do barbers take classes?
2. Why do nurses take classes?
3. What kinds of new skills can people learn?
4. Why do some people take a language course?
5. What kinds of classes can overweight people find?
6. What classes can people take to improve their lives?
7. Where do continuing education classes meet?

** Inferential Questions   Answer these questions. Read the passage again if necessary.

1. How are ideas about education changing?
2. Why is the name "continuing education" a good one?
3. Why would it be better for some people to choose continuing education classes instead of university classes?

What Do You Think?

1. Do the universities or local school systems in your city or country have continuing education classes? If they do, what kinds of classes do they have?
2. What kind of continuing education class would you like to take? Look at the schedule on page 164 for ideas.
3. What new skill would you like to learn?
4. If you were a foreign spouse in the United States, which would be better for you: a university class in English as a second language, or a continuing education class? Why?

VOCABULARY SKILLS

Word Search

1. Write the word in line 6 that means *a chance.*

    _____

2. Write the word in line 11 that means *make larger or greater.*

    _____

3. Write the words in line 21 that mean *emergency help.*

    _____

4. Write the word in lines 24–25 that means *weighing too much.*

    _____

5. Write the word in line 25 that is the *science of food values.*

    _____

6. Write the words in line 26 that mean *be friendly to.*

    _____

7. Write the word in line 32 that means *go to.*

    _____

Idioms and Expressions   *get along with* = be friendly to

> *Examples*
>
> 1. It is important to *get along with* other people.
> 2. He doesn't *get along* well *with* his father-in-law.

Answer these questions:

1. Do you usually get along well with other people?
2. Are you easy to get along with?
3. How do you and your _____ (parents, wife, brother, etc.) get along?
4. What kind of people don't you get along with?
5. Is it important to get along with other people? Why or why not?

∗∗ Vocabulary in Context

attended	continuing education	grades
certificates	exercises	improve
chance	got along	variety

Choose from the listed words and fill in the blanks:

My friend was teaching English as a second language in a _____ class a few years ago. It was a class she enjoyed very much. Most of her students were Japanese women. The classes were important to them for a _____ of reasons. Some went to the class to _____ their English. Others _____ because the class gave them the _____ to see old friends. All the students, even the new ones, _____ together very well. They didn't always do the homework, but they did the _____ in class. They took no tests, and they received no _____. At the end of the semester, they received no _____. However, they had a wonderful party at the end of the semester.

Matching Meanings   These italicized words can have more than one meaning. Match the meaning with each sentence.

      A. unit of temperature   B. university title

___ 1. Did you get your master's *degree* last year?

___ 2. How many *degrees* do you have?

___ 3. It is 10 *degrees* outside this morning.

      A. physical activity   B. mental activity

___ 4. You need to do the *exercise* on page 22 for homework.

___ 5. Overweight people should get more *exercise.*

___ 6. *Exercise* is good for your health.

      A. mark   B. school level

___ 7. Did you get a good *grade* on your exam?

___ 8. Ted is in the fifth *grade.*

___ 9. He needs some good *grades* to go to college.

      A. luck   B. opportunity

___ 10. I only saw him on the street by *chance.*

___ 11. People want the *chance* to improve themselves.

___ 12. He waited for the *chance* to speak to his employer.

      A. kind, sort   B. letters for printing

___ 13. What *type* of exercises are you interested in?

___ 14. He is an outdoor *type* of person.

___ 15. This book is easy to read. It's in large *type.*

READING SKILLS

Pronoun Reference   Draw arrows connecting the circled words to the words they refer to.

Many adults are interested in other kinds of learning. Continuing education gives (them) the opportunity to increase (their) knowledge about their own field or to learn about a new field. (It) also gives (them) a chance to improve their old skills or to learn new (ones).

**Guessing Meanings
from Context**   Choose the best meaning for each italicized word. Use the context to help you.

1. Nurses can take classes to increase their *knowledge.* If they know more or learn more, they can get a better job or earn more money.

   a. learning
   b. helping
   c. earning

2. There is a large *variety* of classes to choose from: typing, foreign cooking, photography, auto repair, furniture repair, or swimming.

   a. choice
   b. change
   c. addition

3. Other adults take continuing education classes to *improve* their own lives, because they want to feel better about themselves.

   a. make . . . possible
   b. increase
   c. make . . . better

Scanning

Continuing Education Classes
Joan Griffith, Adult Education Director
Office Hours: 9:00–1:00
Pre-registration starts September 1 from 9 A.M. to 1 P.M.
For more information, call 233-9800

Course Name	Start Date	Total Hours	Day	Time	Bldg.	Fee
ARTS AND CRAFTS						
Drawing I	Sep 20	20	M	7:00–9:00 PM	High School, Art	22.00
Oil Painting I–IV	Sep 22	20	W	7:00–9:00 PM	Welch Rm 63	22.00
BUSINESS COURSES						
Shorthand	Sep 20	44	MTh	7:00–9:00 PM	High School Rm 110	46.00
Typing I	Sep 20	20	M	7:00–9:00 PM	High School Rm 103	23.00
Typing II	Sep 22	20	W	7:00–9:00 PM	High School Rm 106	23.00
COOKING						
Chinese Cooking	Sep 22	30	W	7:00–10:00 PM	Central Rm 135	33.00 +
Chinese Cooking	Sep 23	30	Th	7:00–10:00 PM	Central Rm 135	33.00 +
French Cooking	Sep 22	24	W	7:00–10:00 PM	High School Rm 17	27.00 +
Mexican Cooking	Sep 23	24	Th	7:00–10:00 PM	High School Rm 17	27.00 +
Microwave, Beg.	Sep 20	15	M	12:30–3:30 PM	2507 Hoover	26.00 +
GENERAL EDUCATION						
Algebra	Sep 22	30	Th	7:00–10:00 PM	High School Rm 108	32.00
Auto Mechanics	Sep 22	30	W	7:00–10:00 PM	High School Rm 4	38.50
Emergency Care	Sep 20	12	M	6:30–9:30 PM	High School Rm 14	19.00
English Grammar Review	Sep 21	15	T	7:00–8:30 PM	High School Rm 110	17.00
Guitar, Beg.	Sep 22	8	W	7:00–8:00 PM	High School Orch. Rm	10.00
Guitar, Inter.	Sep 22	12	W	8:00–9:30 PM	High School Orch. Rm	14.00
Sign Language, Beg.	Sep 21	16	T	7:00–9:00 PM	High School Rm 111	18.00
Sign Language, Beg.	Sep 23	16	Th	7:00–9:00 PM	High School Rm 111	18.00
Small Engine Repair	Sep 20	24	M	7:00–9:00 PM	High School Rm 4	29.00
LANGUAGES						
Arabic, Beg.	Sep 21	24	T	7:00–9:00 PM	High School Rm 121	26.00
German, Beg.	Sep 21	20	T	7:00–9:00 PM	High School Rm 120	22.00
German, Inter.	Sep 22	20	W	7:00–9:00 PM	High School Rm 120	22.00
Spanish, Beg.	Sep 20	30	M	7:00–9:00 PM	High School Rm 122	32.00
Spanish, Inter.	Sep 21	30	T	7:00–9:00 PM	High School Rm 122	32.00
LEISURE						
Dance Exercise	Oct 18	16	MW	6:00–7:00 PM	Central Cafe	18.00
Ballroom Dancing	Sep 21	12	T	7:00–8:30 PM	Central Cafe	14.00
Bellydancing, Beg.	Oct 18	8	M	7:00–8:00 PM	Central Cafe	10.00
Bellydancing, Int.	Oct 20	8	W	7:00–8:00 PM	Central Cafe	10.00
Bridge	Sep 21	20	T	7:00–9:00 PM	High School Rm 105	22.00
Country Western Dance	Sep 23	16	Th	7:00–9:00 PM	Meeker Gym	18.00
Photography	Sep 21	16	T	7:00–9:00 PM	High School Library	24.00
Square Dancing	Sep 21	32	T	7:30–9:30 PM	Northwood Gym	14.00

+ Additional Fee

Scan the variety of continuing education classes listed at left and answer these questions:

1. Where does the Typing I class meet?
2. Where does the Chinese cooking class meet?
3. When does the Beginning Arabic class start?
4. What night does the Auto Mechanics class meet?
5. How many hours a night is the Dance Exercise class?
6. What is the fee for the English Grammar Review?
7. What is the most expensive class?
8. How many hours total is the Beginning Guitar class?
9. What does the symbol + mean?
10. How can you get more information about the classes?
11. When does pre-registration begin?

Main Ideas Choose the main idea. The main idea of

1. paragraph 1 is:

   a. Ideas about education are changing in the United States.
   b. Adults are not interested in going to college.
   c. Education does not end with a diploma.

2. paragraph 3 is:

   a. Secretaries can improve their work skills.
   b. People can take continuing education classes.
   c. People can get better jobs by taking continuing education classes.

3. paragraph 4 is:

   a. Adults can learn new skills.
   b. Adults can choose foreign cooking.
   c. Only some of the classes are available.

4. paragraph 7 is:

   a. Adults have many opportunities to continue their learning.
   b. Adults can continue their learning.
   c. Most classes are in the evening.

READING 2   Read the passage to find out about correspondence schools.

Some people cannot attend a school or a university to continue   1
their education. For them there are radio or TV courses and correspondence courses. These courses are different from regular university courses because the instructor and the student never meet each
other. Everything is done by mail. The schools mail the books and the   5
assignments to the students. Then the students complete the assignments and mail them back to the instructor. The instructor then
checks the assignments for mistakes and at the end of the course,
mails a grade to the student.

Correspondence schools are very popular. They offer courses in   10
more than a thousand subjects, from Arabic to zoology. Today more
than a million Americans are taking some kind of a correspondence
course. Many different kinds of people have graduated from correspondence schools: singers like Donny and Marie Osmond, and even
"Peanuts" cartoonist Charles Schulz.   15

Some correspondence schools have courses to give primary
training for people wanting to get jobs in industry. The Cleveland
Institute of Electronics has courses to help workers get jobs in companies like Eastman Kodak or Procter and Gamble. Some universities have general interest courses or introductory courses. Other   20
universities offer a complete program. The University of Iowa, for
example, offers a Bachelor of Liberal Studies. The courses are general because there is no specific major. To register, students only
have to fill out a registration form and mail it in with a check for
tuition and fees.   25

The costs of correspondence courses vary. Some are very cheap,
and some are very expensive. A typical course costs about $700 or
$900, but some courses can cost as much as $3,000. The program at
the University of Iowa costs about $100 a semester.

The biggest problem with a correspondence course is finishing it.   30
Not everyone completes a course, because working at home can be

difficult and lonely. Students have to read more and write more. Elora McKenzie says, "You must really want to learn because you have to work hard."

Elora McKenzie took a photography correspondence course from 35 the New York Institute of Photography in Manhattan. She lived on a 700-acre sheep farm in West Virginia and couldn't attend the Institute. There were 30 lessons in the course with instructions on cassette tapes. Elora completed each worksheet and mailed it in with her photographs. Professional photographers recorded their ideas on 40 cassette tape and mailed them back to her. "I really enjoyed the work," she says. "It was well organized, and the instruction was very personal." The course was helpful to Elora. She later won a prize in a national photography contest.

COMPREHENSION CHECK

Answer the following questions. You may look back at the passage.

1. How is a correspondence course different from a regular university course?

2. What do correspondence schools offer?

3. What does the University of Iowa offer?

4. What does a student have to do to register for the University of Iowa program?

5. How much do correspondence courses usually cost?

6. What is the biggest problem with correspondence courses?

VOCABULARY SKILLS

Idioms and Expressions   Look at the difference between these two words:

mail = send   I *mailed* a letter to my friend.
mail back = return   The company mailed me the wrong book, so I *mailed* it *back* to them.

We can use the word *back* with other verbs like:

give
take
go
come   } + back = return
pay
send

Answer the following questions. Use a verb + *back*.

1. Your book is overdue at the library. What do you have to do?

_____

2. You ordered a special item from a big company. They sent you the wrong item. What are you going to do?

_____

3. You are on your way to your calculus class and left your textbook at home. What should you do?

_____

4. A friend gave you five dollars until you get a check from home. What will you do when your check arrives?

_____

5. Your car ran out of gas. You saw a gas station about a mile back. What are you going to do?

_____

Word Families   instruction (noun)   During this course, you will receive *instruction* in all types of auto repair.

instructor (noun-person)   Dr. Smith is the *instructor* of the course.
instruct (verb)   Last semester, he *instructed* a class in
  instructed   modern history.
  instructing

Use the listed words to fill in the blanks:

Paul Brown is an _____ at Templar Community College.
He _____ all new students in English composition. He gives
them _____ in punctuation and paragraph writing. He also
gives them a lot of practice in writing compositions. Some of his
students like him. Others think he is a difficult _____.
Mr. Brown doesn't agree. He thinks these students need to listen
more carefully to his _____.

READING SKILLS

Guessing Meanings from Context

Choose the best meaning for each italicized word. Use the context to help you.

1. I'm taking a math course by *correspondence*. Everything is done by mail.
   a. written communication
   b. agreement
   c. an instructor

2. The students complete the *assignments* and mail them back to the instructor.
   a. instructions
   b. homework
   c. examinations

3. The instructor then *checks* the assignments for mistakes.
   a. rewrites
   b. accepts money for
   c. looks over

4. The costs of correspondence courses *vary*. Some are very cheap, and some are very expensive.
   a. are unusual
   b. are typical
   c. are different

Scanning

TV	**TV**
BIOL: 140 TV 3 credits	SPCH: 101 TV 3 credits
INTRODUCTION TO BIOLOGY	FUNDAMENTALS OF SPEECH
CHANNEL 11	CHANNEL D
M–W–F 7:00 A.M.	
Sat. 12:30 & 1:00 P.M.	M–W–F 3:00 P.M.
Sun. 7:00 A.M.	T–W–Th 8:00 P.M.
Sept. 8–Dec. 1	Sept. 13–Dec. 1
The course gives students an understanding of all life forms, from simple plants and animals to the complex system of the human body.	The course gives students knowledge of basic effective communication. Students tape speeches and give them to the instructor for evaluation.
TEXTBOOK $27.95	TEXTBOOKS $12.05
TUITION & FEES $71.50	TUITION & FEES $71.50

Scan the two ads for the TV courses to answer the questions.

1. Are the two TV courses graduate or undergraduate courses?

   _____

   How do you know?

2. How many times can you watch Introduction to Biology during the week?

   _____

3. Which course requires more than one book?

   _____

4. For which course do you pay more for books?

   _____

5. What do students have to do for the speech course?

   _____

CHAPTER REVIEW

1. Give reasons why people take continuing education classes.

_____

_____

2. Describe how continuing education classes are different from university classes.

_____

_____

3. Tell something about correspondence courses.

_____

_____

POST-READING ACTIVITIES

Strip Story Put these sentences in logical order:

___ Students take the final examination.

___ Students register for the course.

___ Students mail the assignments to the instructor.

___ Students watch the lectures on TV.

___ Students buy the books.

___ Students write the assignments.

Word Games The words in the right column each contain the letters IT. Read the clues in the left column and complete the words in the right.

1. things   I T __ __ __

2. room for cooking   __ I T __ __ __ __

3. you eat _____ a fork   __ I T __

4. what a man wears   __ __ I T

5. what you do with a pen   __ __ I T __

6. I'll only be a few minutes.
   _____ for me.   __ __ I T

7. oranges, apples, pears   __ __ __ I T

BEFORE

AFTER

Growing Thin Is Big Business

PRE-READING

Compare the two pictures.
How are they similar, and how are they different?
What is the connection between the two pictures and the title?
What do you think the chapter will be about?

READING 1

Scan the passage to find the answers to these questions:

    1. How many Americans are trying to lose weight?
    2. How many Americans weigh at least 20 percent more than their ideal weight?

Read the passage carefully to learn the answer to this question:

    Why and how are many Americans trying to lose weight?

¹ About 70 million Americans are trying to lose weight. That is almost 1 out of every 3 people in the United States. Some people go on diets. This means they eat less of certain foods, especially fats and sugars. Other people exercise with special equipment, take diet pills, or even have surgery. Losing weight is hard work, and it can also cost a lot of money. So why do so many people in the United States want to lose weight?

² Many people in the United States worry about not looking young and attractive. For many people, looking good also means being thin. Other people worry about their health. Many doctors say being overweight is not healthy. But are Americans really fat?

³ Almost 30 million Americans weigh at least 20 percent more than their ideal weight. In fact, the United States is the most overweight country in the world. "The stored fat of adult Americans weighs 2.3 trillion pounds (1.043 billion kg)," says University of Massachusetts anthropologist George Armelagos. He says burning off that stored energy would produce enough power for 900,000 cars to go 12,000 miles (19,308 km).

⁴ Losing weight is hard work, but most people want to find a fast and easy way to take off fat. Bookstores sell lots of diet books. These books tell readers how to lose weight. Each year, dozens of new books like these are written. Each one promises to get rid of fat.

⁵ Some people diet alone. They say dieting should be private. Other people think, "Misery loves company." They need other people to help them lose weight. Some people join weight-control clubs for this kind of help. One club like this is called Weight Watchers International. The group uses psychology and special diet plans to help its members lose weight. In return, members pay Weight Watchers a fee.

⁶ Losing weight can be expensive. Some overweight people go to   30
elegant spas, like La Costa in California. Men and women may pay
several hundred dollars a day at these spas. Guests live there for a
week or 2, exercise, and eat special low-calorie foods. Breakfast may
only be 200 calories, but it will be beautiful and delicious. After 4
days on the program, one woman lost 5 pounds (2.27 kg). At $400 per   35
day, she spent $320 to lose each pound. But she says it was worth
every penny.

⁷ Spas, books, pills, diets, clubs, and special exercise equipment all
add up to a lot of money. In the United States, losing weight may
mean losing money too.   40

COMPREHENSION CHECK

General Questions   Look at the following statements. Correct them if necessary and add
other ideas from the passage. Follow these examples:

STATEMENT: All Americans are trying to lose weight.

STUDENT 1:   No. Seventy million people are trying to lose
weight.

STUDENT 2:   Almost one out of three people in the United
States is trying to lose weight.

STATEMENT: Some people have operations to lose weight.

STUDENT 1:   Yes. Some people have surgery to lose weight.

1. Some people in the United States diet to lose weight.
2. The United States is the most overweight country in the world.
3. Most bookstores don't sell diet books.
4. "Misery loves company" means when you feel bad, it helps to be
with people who have the same problem.
5. Spas are usually inexpensive places for people to lose weight.
6. In the United States, losing weight can be expensive.

Factual Questions   Answer these questions. You may look back at the passage.

1. What percentage of Americans are trying to lose weight?
2. What do people do to lose weight?
3. Why do many Americans want to lose weight? (two reasons)
4. What do many diet books promise?
5. What is Weight Watchers International? How does it help overweight people?
6. What do people do at spas like La Costa?
7. Why is losing weight sometimes expensive?

** Inferential Questions   Answer these questions. Read the passage again if necessary.

1. What is the connection between looking good and being thin for most people in the United States?
2. What do many American doctors think about fat people?
3. Why do bookstores sell lots of diet books?

What Do You Think?

1. Do people in your home country worry about getting fat? Why or why not? If yes, how do they lose weight?
2. Do you think people in the United States worry too much about gaining weight?
3. Are you surprised to know that Americans spend a lot of money to lose weight? Why or why not?
4. Is there a perfect weight? How do you decide how much someone should weigh?
5. Do you expect to gain weight when you are middle-aged?

VOCABULARY SKILLS

Word Search

1. Write the word in line 3 that means *special plans for eating certain foods.*

   _____

2. Write the word in line 5 that means *medical operation.*

   _____

3. Write the word in line 12 for this sign: %.

   _____

4. Write the word in line 24 that is the opposite of *happiness*.

_____

5. Write the word in line 31 that means *places to go to relax, diet, and exercise*.

_____

6. Write the word in line 34 that means *units to measure energy, especially in foods*.

_____

Opposites   Fill in the blanks with the appropriate word:

Many people in the United States want

(attractive/unattractive)   to look _____. Most Americans

think looking good also means being

(thin/fat)   _____. Some other people also do not

want to be overweight. They say being

(thin/fat)   _____ is not _____. But peo-

(healthy/unhealthy)   ple in the United States do not want to

work hard to take off weight. So when

(lose/gain)   they _____ weight, they look for

(easy/hard)   _____ ways to lose it.

Affixes   The prefix *over-* has several meanings. One common meaning is "too much" or "too long."

Examples

1. He is *over*weight. = He weighs *too much.*

2. Don't *over*sleep or you'll be late for class. } = { Don't sleep *too long.*

Read these sentences. Use the context to help you decide the meaning of the italicized word. Then write the meaning in the space provided.

1. Don't *overfeed* the dog or it will be sick.

   _____

2. He *overspent* his salary and now he has no money.

   _____

3. Guests should not *overstay* their welcome with their host or hostess.

   _____

4. I think the waitress *overcharged* us for our meal. Let's add up the bill again.

   _____

5. That fruit is *overripe.* I don't think it will be good to eat.

   _____

The affix *-ist* often means "a person who is a specialist or expert in a certain area." Look at the following examples. Follow these patterns and complete the chart. Add your own examples in the spaces.

Subject	Meaning	Person
1. anthropology	the study of humans	anthropologist
2. geology	the study of the earth, rocks, minerals, etc.	_____
3. psychology	the study of human behavior	_____
4. dentistry	care of the teeth	dentist
5. linguistics	the study of language	_____
6. biology	the study of life	_____
7. chemistry	_____	_____
8. _____	the study of human society	_____

	Subject	*Meaning*	*Person*
9.	_____	_____	_____
10.	_____	_____	_____
11.	_____	_____	_____

READING SKILLS

Connections   Connect the underlined word or groups of words to the ideas they refer to. Refer to the example on page 85 if necessary.

1. Bookstores sell lots of diet books. <u>These books</u> tell readers how to lose weight. Each year, dozens of new books like <u>these</u> are written. <u>Each one of them</u> promises to get rid of fat.

2. Other people think, "Misery loves company." <u>They</u> need other people to help them lose weight. Some people join weight-control clubs for <u>this kind</u> of help. One club <u>like this</u> is called Weight Watchers International. The <u>group</u> uses psychology and special diet plans to help <u>its</u> members lose weight.

Main Ideas   Choose the main idea. The main idea of

1. paragraph 1 is:
   a. Many people are overweight.
   b. Some people use special equipment.
   c. Many Americans are trying to lose weight.

2. paragraph 3 is:
   a. The United States is the most overweight country in the world.
   b. The stored fat of adult Americans weighs 2.3 trillion pounds.
   c. George Armelagos is an anthropologist at the University of Massachusetts.

3. paragraph 6 is:
   a. Some overweight people go to spas.
   b. Losing weight can be expensive.
   c. Breakfast at a spa may only be 200 calories.

4. the whole passage is:
   a. Overweight Americans worry about not looking young and attractive.
   b. Some doctors say being overweight is not healthy.
   c. Overweight people in the United States may spend a lot of money losing weight.

READING 2

Read this passage to learn more about the diet club, Weight Watchers.

Jean Nidetch and Albert Lippert were fat, but they are not now. [1]
Nidetch lost 72 pounds (32.66 kg) and started an organization called
Weight Watchers. Weight Watchers is a club to help people lose
weight. Albert Lippert lost 40 pounds (18.14 kg) and later became
president of Weight Watchers. Lippert says Weight Watchers is not [5]
just a "fat club." It is an organization to help people learn new eating
habits. People learn how and what to eat. They learn how to eat well
without getting fat.

Weight Watchers is more than just a club. There are Weight
Watchers restaurants, low-calorie frozen foods, cookbooks, a maga- [10]
zine, and several camps for overweight children. But most importantly, Weight Watchers is an educational organization. Weight
Watchers holds 12,000 weekly classes around the world. These
classes help members learn how to change their eating habits and
lose weight. Instructors teach club members tricks to help them stay [15]
on their diets. Here is one trick: Eat food off a small plate instead of
a big one. A small amount of food on a small plate looks like more
than a small amount of food on a large plate.

Weight Watchers is a successful business because many people
lose weight with its help. Today Al Lippert is president of a multi- [20]
million dollar company. There are Weight Watcher clubs in Canada,
Mexico, Western Europe, and Australia. How does Al Lippert feel
about his life and his job? "I love working with Weight Watchers, and
I enjoy life. It's simple, really. Fat people are not happy."

COMPREHENSION CHECK

Answer these questions. You may look back at the passage.

1. What is Weight Watchers?
2. Who is Jean Nidetch?
3. Who is Albert Lippert?
4. What happens at Weight Watchers classes?
5. Why is Weight Watchers a successful business?
6. What does Lippert say about overweight people? Do you agree with him?

VOCABULARY SKILLS

Word Families

education (noun)	I want a good *education*.
educator (noun-person)	He is an *educator*.
educate (verb) educated educating	They want to *educate* their son at Harvard.
educated (adjective)	She is an *educated* person.

Use the listed words to fill in the blanks:

I received a good _____, and today I am a professional _____. I have two children, and I hope to _____ my children at good universities. When they are adults, I want them to be _____ persons.

organization (noun)	She belongs to several professional *organizations*.
organizer (noun-person)	He is a good political *organizer*.
organize (verb) organized organizing	It takes a long time to *organize* a house.
organized (adjective)	My secretary is an *organized* person.

Use the listed words to fill in the blanks:

I am not an _____ person, but I would like to be. One year I tried to _____ my desk and bookshelves. I even joined an _____ that promised it could help me become _____. It didn't help. My office is still a mess.

READING SKILLS

Guessing Meanings from Context Choose the best meaning for each italicized word. Use the context to help you.

1. Nidetch lost weight and started an organization called Weight Watchers. Weight Watchers is a *club* to help people lose weight.
   a. a big stick
   b. an organization of people
   c. a weight program

2. Instructors teach club members tricks to help them stay on their diets. Here is one *trick:* Eat food off a small plate instead of a big one.
   a. something to fool someone
   b. a unit in a card game
   c. something instructors do to students

3. Some people go on *diets.* This means they eat less of certain foods, especially fats and sugars.
   a. programs that limit what one eats
   b. governing bodies
   c. food

4. It is an organization to help people learn new eating *habits.* People learn how and what to eat.
   a. drug problems
   b. usual customs
   c. special kinds of dress

Pronoun Reference Draw arrows connecting the circled words to the words they refer to.

Jean Nidetch and Albert Lippert were once fat, but (they) aren't now. Jean started an organization called Weight Watchers, and Albert is (its) president. It is an organization to help people learn new eating habits. (They) learn how to eat well without getting fat. Classes help members learn how to change (their) eating habits.

Scanning

> ## Low-Calorie Menu
>
> | *Breakfast* | *Calories* |
> | --- | --- |
> | whole wheat toast | 56 |
> | boiled egg | 81 |
> | orange juice, small glass | 89 |
> | coffee or tea | 0 |
>
> | *Lunch* | |
> | --- | --- |
> | smoked salmon | 100 |
> | tomato soup | 86 |
> | whole wheat toast | 56 |
> | fresh strawberries ½ cup) | 28 |
> | coffee or tea | 0 |
>
> | *Dinner* | |
> | --- | --- |
> | broiled chicken without skin | 155 |
> | cucumber | 45 |
> | baked potato with butter | 150 |
> | fresh pear | 100 |
> | coffee or tea | 0 |

Scan this typical low-calorie diet menu to find the answers to these questions.

1. Which fruit has fewer calories?
   a. a pear
   b. ½ cup of strawberries

2. Which has more calories?
   a. a small glass of orange juice
   b. tomato soup

3. Which meal has more calories?
   a. breakfast
   b. dinner

4. Which has more calories?
   a. smoked salmon
   b. broiled chicken

5. Which meal includes strawberries for dessert?
   a. lunch
   b. dinner

That La Costa Look
Come to where it all began.

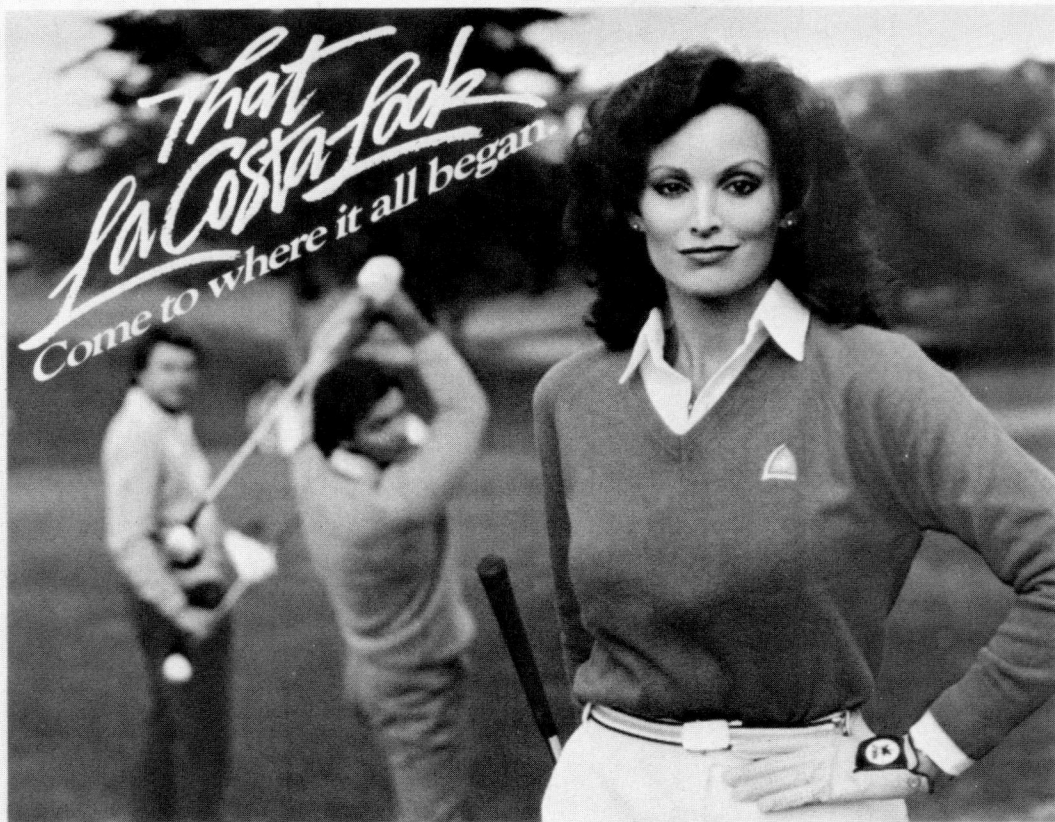

For golfers who care about value.

You can stay at La Costa with meals and green fees for about $115 per day.*

That La Costa Look is you, looking and feeling your very best. It comes from the many things to do at La Costa, like tennis at our Racquet Club, and friendly atmosphere which brings our guests back to La Costa, again and again.

25 courts, plus practice lanes. You'll love our golf courses, superb restaurants and numerous activities. Our famous spa offers the option of countless pleasures such as a massage or facial. But mostly, you'll enjoy the casual, warm

See your travel agent or call us toll-free for information, brochures or reservations: 800-854-6564. In California: 800-542-6200. Or write: La Costa Hotel & Spa, Carlsbad, CA 92008.

*Per person, per day, double occupancy, includes breakfast and dinner.

LA COSTA
HOTEL & SPA
THE COMPLETE RESORT

Look at the ad for a spa at left and answer these questions:

1. What is the name of the spa?
2. How many tennis courts are there?
3. What kind of activities are there?
4. How much does it cost to stay at this resort?
5. Where can you write for information?
6. How else can you get information about this resort?

CHAPTER REVIEW

1. Use the spaces to write what you might eat on a typical day:

   Breakfast _____

   _____

   _____

   Lunch _____

   _____

   _____

   Dinner _____

   _____

   _____

2. If you ever have a snack (something to eat between meals), write your typical snack here:

   _____

   _____

3. List ways people use to lose weight:

   _____

   _____

   _____

   _____

POST-READING ACTIVITY

Word Search Puzzle   Fill in the blanks with words opposite in meaning of the listed words. Then find the opposites in the puzzle. The words can go forward, backward, up, down, or diagonally.

artificial	*real*	receive	_____
expensive	_____	new	_____
first	_____	private	_____
forget	_____	sell	_____
important	_____	useful	_____
keep	_____	usual	_____
learn	_____	young	_____
loudly	_____	easy	_____
thin	_____	lose	_____

```
H  A  R  D  I  G  C  T  R  N  U
T  N  A  T  R  O  P  M  I  N  U
H  U  Z  R  E  L  E  A  R  N  S
R  S  T  S  A  L  G  E  U  G  E
O  F  E  O  L  D  B  S  T  O  L
W  U  A  R  T  M  U  G  I  V  E
A  L  C  H  E  A  P  E  H  C  S
W  E  H  M  L  Y  L  T  F  O  S
A  E  E  Z  B  U  S  E  D  A  N
Y  R  X  P  U  B  L  I  C  E  T
```

One Day at a Time

PRE-READING

How old do you think the man in the picture is?

The man is now retired. What do you think the man's occupation was?

READING 1

Scan the passage to find the answers to these questions:

1. When was the man born?
2. How much did he sell his shop for?
3. How big was the ranch in Cooper?

Read the passage carefully to learn the answer to this question:

Why does the man say he's independent?

[1] Older people in the United States have a variety of life-styles. Some live with their children, some live in nursing homes, and some live alone. In the following passage, Lon, an old man, tells his story:

[2] "I am an independent kind of person. I guess it's because I was born on Independence Day, July 4, 1889, in Texas. I guess it's also because I always did things my own way. My father, for example, was a cotton farmer, but I didn't want to become a farmer, so I became a rancher instead.

[3] I wanted to attend Baylor University in Texas. Baylor wanted me on their football team, but my father wouldn't pay the tuition money for me to play football. So I paid for my own college education. To get money for books and tuition, a friend and I bought an old clothes press shop. We each paid $15. We pressed suits and jackets, and made minor repairs during our 4 years of college. When I graduated in 1911, I sold my half of the shop for $5000.

[4] After college, I worked for the American Fruit Company. My first job was in Honduras where I worked as a timekeeper and made $70 a month. The Company then sent me to Guatemala. There I worked as a farm manager and earned $700 a month.

[5] Most people would keep a good job like that, but not I. During World War I, I gave up my job and joined the Army. Suddenly I was earning only $15 a month as an ordinary soldier. However, near the end of the war, I became the commander of a military unit. We made bread for the soldiers in Europe.

[6] After the war, I returned to Texas and bought a 2000-acre (810 ha) ranch in Cooper. I paid $50 an acre for the ranch, and I raised cattle, sheep, pigs, and goats on it.

[7] In those days most ranchers let their cattle go freely over the open land, but I didn't. I put a fence° around my ranch. This fence caused me a lot of trouble with my neighbors. They would cut my

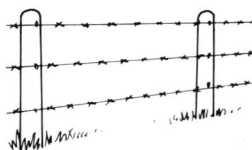

Fence

fence and steal my animals. After they killed 17 of my horses, I 30
followed their tracks.° I talked to the leader of the troublemakers. I
told him I would have to use my gun if he didn't stop making trouble.
I guess he understood me, because he moved to another town.

⁸ Then I met Ruby Goble, a pretty schoolteacher in the next
town. In 1926, we decided to get married, but her father wasn't
happy about the idea because I was 15 years older. At that time I was 35
37, and she was only 22. Her father was afraid I'd die and leave her
with a bunch of children to raise.

⁹ Humph! My father was 94 when he died, and my mother was
97, so I expected to live a long time. When I told this to Ruby's father,
he changed his mind about me, and said I could be his son-in-law. 40
Ruby and I got married, and in addition to raising cattle, sheep, pigs,
and goats, we began to raise boys—4 of them. When my youngest son
was born, I was 50 years old."

Tracks

COMPREHENSION CHECK

General Questions

Look at the following statements. Correct them if necessary and add
other ideas from the passage.

1. The man says he is independent.
2. He didn't go to college.
3. Lon always had a good job.
4. After the war, he bought a ranch in Texas.
5. The man was younger than his wife.
6. Lon and Ruby raised only cattle.

Factual Questions

Answer these questions. You may look back at the passage.

1. Where did the man get the money for his college education?
2. Where did he work after college?
3. Why did he quit his job in Guatemala?
4. What was he doing near the end of the war?
5. What did he do after the war?
6. How much did he pay for his ranch in Cooper?
7. How did his neighbors give him a lot of trouble?
8. Whom did he want to marry?
9. What was the difference in their ages?
10. How old were the man's parents when they died?

∗∗ Inferential Questions   Answer the questions. Read the passage again if necessary.

1. How much did the man and his friend pay for the clothes press shop?
2. Was the man's clothes press business successful?
3. Where is Cooper?
4. Why did the man's neighbors cut his fences and steal his animals?
5. How strongly was Ruby's father against her marriage?

What Do You Think?   1. How long do people in your country usually live?
2. Who is the oldest person you know? How old is he or she? What reason does he or she give for such a long life?
3. Why do some people live a long time?

VOCABULARY SKILLS

Word Search   1. Write the word in line 8 that means *in place of.*

_____

2. Write the word in line 10 that means *payment for instruction.*

_____

3. Write the word in line 13 that means *to iron.*

_____

4. Write the word in line 26 that means *cows and bulls.*

_____

5. Write the word in line 32 that means *footprints.*

_____

6. Write the word in line 40 that means *take care of.*

_____

Idioms and Expressions   *get married* = to become married

Examples

get married to + NAME   Lon *got married to* Ruby.
get married in + TIME/PLACE   They *got married* in 1926.

Answer these questions:

1. Are you married? If yes, when did you get married?
2. At what age do people in your country usually get married?
3. Where do people usually get married? What do they wear?
4. How do people celebrate when they get married?

Word Families

graduation (noun)	After his *graduation,* he got a job in Honduras.
graduate (noun-person)	He's a high school *graduate.*
graduate (verb) graduated graduating	He *graduated* from Baylor in 1911.

Use the listed words to fill in the blanks:

Mike will _____ from Taylor University next spring. He is the only college _____ in his family. His parents and his sister _____ from high school, but they never went to college. Mike's father wants him to work in the family store after _____, but Mike isn't interested. He wants to go to _____ school in the fall and study biochemistry.

Opposites Fill in the blanks with the appropriate word.

(major/minor)

1. Susan graduated last year with a B.A. in education. Her _____ was education.

(oldest/youngest)

2. Uncle Fred is 102 years old. He is the _____ person in our family.

(dependent/independent)

3. Joan is 17 years old and has a job and an apartment. She doesn't need anyone. She's very _____.

(bored/interested)   4. There's nothing good on TV. I don't have anything to read, and I can't think of anything good to do. I'm _____.

(leader/follower)   5. In one children's game, one child is the _____. She does something, and the other children copy her.

READING SKILLS

Connections   Connect the underlined word or groups of words to the idea they refer to. Refer to the example on page 85 if necessary.

1. Older people in the United States have a variety of life-styles. <u>Some</u> live with their children, and some live alone.
2. The company then sent me to Guatemala. <u>There</u> I worked as a farm manager.
3. I worked as a farm manager and earned $700 a month. Most people would keep a good job like <u>that</u>, but not I.
4. I expected to live a long time. When I told <u>this</u> to Ruby's father, he changed his mind about me.
5. In 1927, we decided to get married. <u>At that time</u>, I was 37, and she was only 22.

Main Ideas   Choose the main idea. The main idea of

1. paragraph 1 is:
   a. Some people live alone.
   b. Old people live differently.
   c. One old man tells his story.

2. paragraph 3 is:
   a. The man paid for his own college education.
   b. The man played on the Baylor football team.
   c. The man became rich.

3. paragraph 7 is:
   a. The man had a big ranch.
   b. The man had problems with his neighbors.
   c. The man built fences.

4. paragraph 8 is:
   a. Lon met Ruby Goble.
   b. Ruby's father thought Lon was too old to marry her.
   c. Ruby was a pretty school teacher.

READING 2

Read the passage carefully to learn the answer to this question:

   Why did Lon retire?

"In 1944 I moved my family to Bristol, Texas, because I wanted   1
to be near my parents. I didn't sell my farm in Cooper, but bought
another one in Bristol. After my parents died, I sold the Bristol farm
and moved to Commerce. There I bought a 75-acre (30.38 ha) farm,
because it was near my ranch and because I wanted a small place for   5
my retirement. I tried to grow cotton and vegetables on my farm, but
I wasn't very successful.

Then, in 1968, at 78 years of age, I sold the Texas ranch and
bought a 3000-acre (1215 ha) ranch in Venezuela. My wife and two
of my sons and their wives went with me. We took the farm equipment and the animals with us. Five years later, Ruby and I left   10
Venezuela and returned to our small farm in Commerce. She was ill,
and I was 82 and ready to retire.

In 1977, Ruby died, and I became independent again. I have 4
sons, 13 grandchildren, and 3 great-grandchildren, but I live alone.
One son lives only 5 hours from me, and I see him several times a   15
month. The others I see only once or twice a year.

My days, however, are full. I usually get up at 5:30 in the morning, feed and milk the goats, feed the chickens, and collect the
eggs. Then I fix breakfast. After breakfast, there are always other
chores to do: working in the garden, repairing fences, or working in   20
the house.

In the spring, I plant a large garden with strawberries, corn,
beans, squash, and potatoes. I sell most of the strawberries and freeze
the rest. I also freeze most of the vegetables. Behind my house, there

is a small lake. I let people fish there for a dollar a day. This gives me
a little money and some company.   25

Once a week, I drive into town and run errands. I go to the post
office, the bank, and the supermarket. Then, on Sundays, I go to
church. All my friends visit me often. I guess they are worried about
me because I'm so old and live alone.

But I'm not worried. My mind and my appetite are still good. I   30
may be retired, but I have a lot of things to do. I know one day I will
die, but I don't worry about that. Instead, I live and enjoy just one
day at a time."

**COMPREHENSION
CHECK**

Answer these questions:

1. Why did Lon buy the farm in Commerce?
2. Why did he leave Venezuela?
3. How does he spend his days?
4. How does he get money?
5. Does he stay on the farm everyday?
6. How does Lon feel about living alone?

VOCABULARY SKILLS

Compound Words   **One-Word Forms**

Follow this example:

What do you call a person who teaches school?

a schoolteacher

What do you call a person who:

keeps time? _____   makes trouble? _____

keeps the books? _____   owns a home? _____

washes dishes? _____

Two-Word Forms

Follow this example:

What do you call a person who manages a farm?

a farm manager

washes windows? ＿＿＿＿＿＿   picks strawberries? ＿＿＿＿＿＿

earns wages? ＿＿＿＿＿＿   smokes cigarettes? ＿＿＿＿＿＿

makes bread? ＿＿＿＿＿＿   plays basketball? ＿＿＿＿＿＿

plays cards? ＿＿＿＿＿＿   plays the trumpet? ＿＿＿＿＿＿

✱✱ Vocabulary in Context

company	independent	retire
farm	old	
plant	worried about	

Choose from the listed words to fill in the blanks:

Next week I'll ＿＿＿＿＿＿ from the North Star Company. My family is ＿＿＿＿＿＿ me. They want me to move in with them, but I prefer to be more ＿＿＿＿＿＿. I may be ＿＿＿＿＿＿, but I'm not helpless. I want to buy a small one- or two-acre ＿＿＿＿＿＿. I want to have a small vegetable garden and ＿＿＿＿＿＿ only my favorite vegetables. I know my family will want to visit me often and I'll enjoy their ＿＿＿＿＿＿.

READING SKILLS

Guessing Meanings from Context

Choose the best meaning for each italicized word. Use the context to help you.

1. Once a week, I drive into town and *run some errands.* I go to the bank and to the post office to collect my mail. On the way home, I stop at the supermarket.
   a. take part in something
   b. take a short trip to do something necessary
   c. go to work

2. My days, however, are *full.* I usually get up at 5:30 in the morning, feed and milk the goats, feed the chickens, and collect the eggs.
a. fat
b. long
c. busy

3. After breakfast, there are always other *chores* to do: working in the garden, repairing fences, or washing dishes.
a. little jobs around the house
b. work in the garden
c. work in the house

Connections   Connect the underlined word or groups of words to the idea they refer to. Refer to the example on page 85 if necessary.

1. I sold the Bristol farm and moved to Commerce. <u>There</u> I bought a 75-acre farm.

2. I have 4 sons, 13 grandchildren, and 3 great-grandchildren. One son lives only five hours from me, and I see him several times a month. The <u>others</u> I see only once or twice a year.

3. I sell most of the strawberries and freeze the <u>rest</u>.

4. Behind my house is a small lake. I let people fish <u>there</u> for a dollar a day.

Connecting Words   Look at these sentences:

1. *After* college, I worked in Honduras.
2. *After* the war was over, I bought a ranch.

Match the phrases in Column A with Column B.

Column A	*Column B*
g 1. After the war was over,	a. I lived alone.
___ 2. After Ruby and I got married,	b. my wife died.
___ 3. After breakfast,	c. I sell some and freeze some.
___ 4. After dinner,	d. I read a little and then go to bed.
___ 5. Four years after I returned from Venezuela,	e. we had four sons.
___ 6. After my wife died,	f. I work in my garden.
___ 7. After I pick the strawberries,	g. I bought a ranch.

CHAPTER REVIEW

1. Give examples of Lon's independence.

_____

_____

_____

2. Describe his different occupations.

_____

_____

_____

3. Describe Lon's retired life.

_____

_____

_____

**POST-READING
ACTIVITIES**

This is Lon's linear biography. It shows the important events in his life.

Born   Graduated   Bought ranch   Got married   Youngest son born   Moved to Bristol   Bought farm   Bought ranch in Venezuela   Wife died   Celebrated 94th birthday

1889   1911   1925   1926   1939   1944   1952   1968   1977   1983

Fill out your own linear biography:

Word Search Puzzle   Look at this list of words and try to find them in the word puzzle.
NOTHING GOES DOWN OR ACROSS

beans	chickens	strawberries
corn	squash	potatoes
cows	goats	cotton
pigs	sheep	horses
		children

```
N  O  C  E  C  S  P  S  H  E  E  S
S  R  O  H  G  H  E  O  G  S  E  A
N  R  O  O  I  P  I  S  T  I  A  W
P  L  A  C  E  C  O  L  R  Q  P  B
A  T  E  E  O  Y  K  R  D  O  U  E
S  O  H  W  S  T  E  E  T  R  H  R
I  S  S  N  Q  B  T  A  N  E  E  S
B  I  N  T  W  Y  T  O  Q  S  Q  N
L  W  O  A  R  O  L  T  N  U  U  V
U  Y  R  M  E  P  J  A  A  M  S  L
R  T  L  S  J  B  W  S  H  E  R  N
S  Q  U  L  R  T  H  T  O  R  E  Y
```

14

A Yankee Clambake

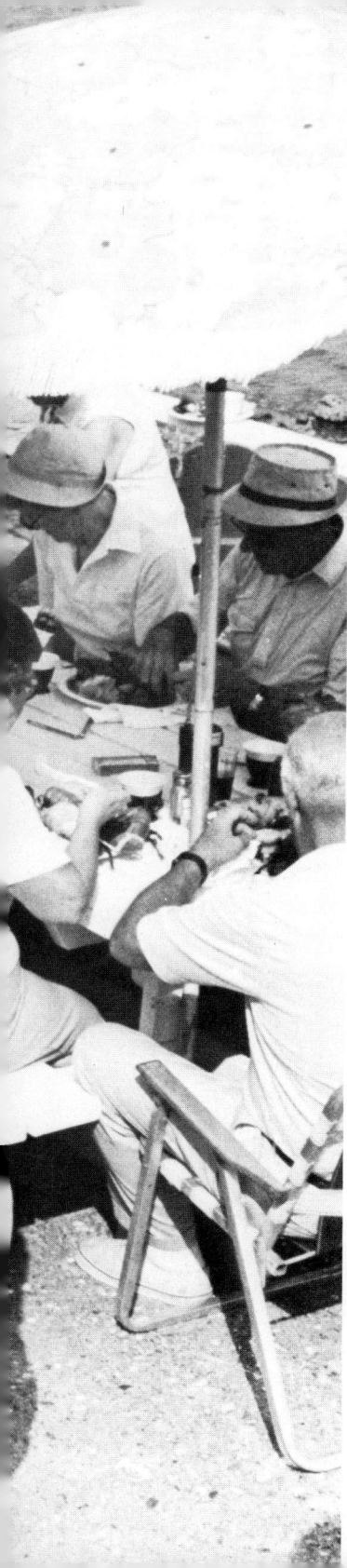

PRE-READING

What are the people in the picture doing?
Where is the activity taking place?
What time of the year do you think it is? Why?

READING 1 Scan this passage to find the answers to these questions:

1. What is the name of one of the biggest and most famous clambakes in New England?
2. How many people work to prepare the clambake?

Read the passage carefully to learn more about clambakes.

Clams

¹ Texas has its chili, and California has its fruits and vegetables. 1
Philadelphia is famous for its ice cream, and Milwaukee is famous for
its beer. But in the northeast corner of the United States, called New
England, seafood is the specialty. The traditional way to eat this
seafood in New England is at a clambake. 5

² A clambake is a giant picnic. Clambakes are usually in late summer. Clams° are the main food, but there is also corn, potatoes, beer,
brown bread, and clam chowder. Chowder is a thick soup which is
made of fish or clams, milk, and vegetables. Sometimes there may
also be clamcakes and sausage and, for dessert, watermelon. 10

³ One of the biggest and most famous clambakes in New England
is the Moosup Valley Grange Clambake in Foster, Rhode Island. This
tradition began more than 50 years ago. In the beginning, it was a
private event, but today the clambake is open to the public. Almost
1000 people buy tickets to it each year. Almost nobody in Foster, 15
Rhode Island wants to miss this event.

⁴ The clambake takes 100 people 2 days to prepare. Workers prepare about 500 sweet and white potatoes, 200 pounds of fish (90.72
kg), 65 dozen ears of corn, and of course, lots of clams.

⁵ There are 2 fires for cooking. Each one is 6 feet high (183.9 cm) 20
and 8 feet long (243.8 cm) and made of wood and rocks. After the
wood burns, workers push the hot rocks to the center and put lots
of rockweed° on the rocks. (The rockweed will give the food a special
flavor.) Next, they put the clams, potatoes, and corn on the rocks.

Rockweed

Finally, several people quickly put heavy, wet bags over the pile and   25
then cover everything with big pieces of wet canvas.

⁶ About 80 minutes after the baking begins, the chef looks at his
watch and says, "It's time to eat." A fire truck comes and puts water
on the fire. Smoke and steam rise. A photographer takes a picture of
the event. Then, men and boys, who are wearing rubber gloves, run   30
up, pull off the canvas, and begin to uncover dinner. Younger helpers, boys and girls, run with their baskets to the 15 crowded tables.
Lots of hungry people are waiting.

⁷ People eat and eat and eat. When their plates are empty, someone fills them up again. At the end of the meal, many people hold   35
their hands to their stomachs and say they cannot eat any more.

⁸ But a clambake is more than good food. It is time to talk and
laugh, to see old friends and neighbors, and to make new friends.
Nobody wants to miss the clambake. Says one man who takes part
every year, "The only reason to miss the clambake is if you're sick   40
or dying."

HISTORICAL NOTE

Fifty years may seem like a short time for a tradition, but clambakes are really
much older. Indians taught the first white people in northeast America to
cook clams, potatoes, and corn in this way.

Indians used wood, rocks, and rockweed and put a cover over the fire. This
made a kind of steam cooker. They taught this cooking method to the white
people. Their great-great-grandchildren are still using a similar method at
clambakes today.

COMPREHENSION
CHECK

General Questions   Look at the following statements: Correct them if necessary and add other ideas from the passage.

1. Philadelphia is famous for ice cream.
2. Clambakes are usually in winter.
3. Nearly a hundred people buy tickets to the Moosup Valley Grange Clambake each year.
4. Many people help prepare for the clambake.
5. Most people eat lots of food at clambakes.
6. The Moosup Valley Grange Clambake is a tradition.

Factual Questions   Answer these questions. You may look back at the passage.

1. How do people traditionally eat seafood in New England?
2. What is the typical food at a clambake?
3. What is chowder?
4. How many people come to the clambake each year?
5. How do people prepare for the clambake?
6. How are the fires prepared?
7. What happens when the food is ready?
8. What do the younger helpers do?
9. What happens when your plate is empty?
10. What do many people do at the end of the meal?
11. What do people do at clambakes besides eat?
12. What does one man say is the only reason to miss the clambake?

** Inferential Questions   Answer these questions. Read the passage again if necessary.

1. Why does almost everyone in Foster, Rhode Island, want to go to the clambake?
2. Why do workers wear rubber gloves to uncover dinner?
3. Why do people hold their hands to their stomachs at the end of the meal?

What Do You Think?   1. Do you think the United States is a country without traditions?
2. What is the most important traditional celebration in your town?
3. Why do you think most people enjoy traditions?
4. What food is the specialty of your town or country?

VOCABULARY SKILLS

Word Search

1. Write the word in line 7 that means *shellfish from the ocean used as food.*

   _____

2. Write the word in line 8 that means *thick soup made with clams or fish, milk, and vegetables.*

   _____

3. Write the word in line 17 that means almost the same as *make.*

   _____

4. Write the word in line 19 that means *twelve of something.*

   _____

5. Write the word in line 23 that means *a kind of plant that grows in the sea.*

   _____

6. Write the word in line 26 that means *a strong cloth used for tents, sails, and bags.*

   _____

7. Write the word in line 27 that means *the main cook.*

   _____

8. Write the word in line 32 that means *having little space to move.*

   _____

Compound Words   **One-Word Forms**

Look at this example:

   shellfish = shell + fish
   A shellfish is a sea animal with a shell around it.

Write the compound word for each meaning:

1. A special dinner with baked clams as the main dish.

   _____

2. A fried cake made with clams.

   _____

3. A weed which grows on rocks in the sea.

   _____

4. A melon with lots of juice (like water) inside.

   _____

5. A book that tells how to cook.

   _____

6. Land for farming.

   _____

7. A book used as a text.

   _____

8. A game played by kicking a ball with the foot.

   _____

READING SKILLS

Pronoun Reference   At clambakes, people eat and eat and eat. When (their) plates are empty, someone fills (them) up again. At the end of the meal, people hold their hands to their stomachs and say (they) cannot eat any more.

Main Idea   Choose the main idea. The main idea of

1. paragraph 1 is:
   a. Texas has chili.
   b. The United States has famous food.
   c. Each part of the United States has its special foods.

2. paragraph 4 is:
   a. Preparing for the clambake is a big job.
   b. There is a lot of corn at the clambake.
   c. People work at clambakes.

3. paragraph 8 is:
   a. Clambakes are good places to eat, talk, and enjoy yourself.
   b. Clambakes are mostly for food.
   c. Even sick people don't like to miss clambakes.

READING 2

Read the passage carefully to learn the answer to this question:

What is chili and the tradition behind it?

Nobody really knows who first made chili, but Texans probably 1
started eating it at least 100 years ago. In 1977, chili became the state
dish of Texas. To make chili, cooks cut beef into small pieces, then
they combine the beef with hot chili peppers, garlic, and other
spices. Chili is thicker than soup and traditionally served in a heavy 5
china bowl and eaten with a spoon. Some cooks add onions, tomatoes,
and additional spices. Many cooks also add beans to the mixture, but
in Texas this is not traditional.

Lots of people think chili is Mexican, but this is not true. Some
people say an angry cook made the first chili. The story says he was 10
a mean man who cooked for cowboys. One day the cowboys complained to him. They said the meat was too tough to eat. So he
chopped it into small pieces and put on enough pepper to burn their
mouths. To his surprise, the cowboys liked it.

Chili became popular outside of Texas during the Great Depres- 15
sion. Many people were poor during this time, and chili was cheap
and filled their stomachs. It grew in popularity in the 1960s when the
United States had a president from Texas. Lyndon Johnson loved
chili and ate it often at the White House.

Today chili is one of the most popular of all American foods, 20
especially in Texas. Texans started a chili society in Dallas in 1939.

In 1967, they held their first chili-making contest in Terlingua, Texas. After that, thousands of people became interested in chili contests. In 1975, former Texans who were living in California started their own International Chili Society and began to organize an annual contest. In 1979, more than 30,000 people attended this event. 25

Today, you can probably get chili almost everywhere in the United States. No two chilis will taste exactly alike. Some will have tomatoes, some will have beans, and others will have only meat and spices. But one thing is certain: the closer you get to Texas, the hotter the chili will be. 30

COMPREHENSION CHECK

Answer these questions. You may look back at the passage.

1. What does Texas-style chili contain?
2. Tell the story of the first chili.
3. When did chili become popular outside of Texas?
4. Who was the U.S. president who loved chili?
5. What kind of event does the International Chili Society hold each year?
6. As you move closer to Texas, what happens to the chili?

VOCABULARY SKILLS

Word Families

specialty (noun)   Chili is the *speciality* of many Texas cooks.
specialize (verb)   I'm going to *specialize* in chemical engineering.
    specialized
    specializing
special (adjective)   Certain students have *special* problems with English grammar.

Use the listed words to fill in the blanks:

Chili is the _____ of this restaurant. Sam, the head cook, is

from Texas, and most Texas cooks like to think they make very

_____ chili. Sam's recipe for chili is his mother's, and, of

course, she _____ in chili making too.

cooker (noun)	We cooked the rice in a special *cooker*.
cooking (noun)	*Cooking* is fun with good *cooking* utensils.
cook (noun-person)	Bill is a *cook* at a neighborhood restaurant.
cook (verb)	I *cook* my dinner when I come home.
cooked	
cooking	

Use the listed words to fill in the blanks:

Some _____ like to prepare certain foods in a special piece of equipment called a pressure _____. The food _____ with steam under pressure so it _____ much faster than by the usual _____ method.

READING SKILLS

Guessing Meanings from Context

Choose the best meaning for each italicized word. Use the context to help you.

1. Texas-style chili is beef *chopped* into small pieces combined with hot chili peppers, garlic, and other spices.
   a. cut
   b. mixed
   c. dried

2. One day the cowboys *complained* to him. They said the meat was too tough to eat.
   a. said something was bad
   b. said something was good
   c. said they were sorry

3. They said the meat was too *tough* to eat. So he chopped it into small pieces and poured on enough pepper to burn their mouths.
   a. hard
   b. old
   c. salty

4. In 1975, *former* Texans living in California started their own chili society and began to organize annual contests.
   a. people who farm
   b. people who are no longer . . .
   c. younger

Sentence Splitting   Look at this example:

> Chowder is a thick soup which is made of fish or clams, and vegetables.

This sentence contains two sentences:

1. Chowder is a thick soup.
2. Chowder is made of fish or clams, and vegetables.

Split the sentences below.

A. Then, men and boys, who are wearing rubber gloves, run up, pull off the canvas, and begin to dig out dinner.

    1. _____

    2. _____

    3. _____

    4. _____

B. The story says he was a mean man who cooked for cowboys.

    1. _____

    2. _____

C. Then in 1975, former Texans who were living in California started the International Chili Society.

    1. _____

      _____

    2. _____

      _____

CHAPTER REVIEW

1. In your own words, tell what happens at a clambake.

_____

_____

_____

2. Tell how to make Texas-style chili.

_____

_____

_____

POST-READING ACTIVITIES

Strip Story   Put the following sentences in logical order:

___ Workers put rockweed and clams, potatoes, and corn on the rocks.

___ The wood burns.

___ Workers push the hot rocks to the center.

___ One hundred people work for two days to prepare the clambake.

___ Workers build fires with wood and rocks.

___ A fire truck puts water on the fire.

___ Workers fill the children's baskets with food.

___ People cover everything with big pieces of wet canvas.

___ Men and boys uncover dinner.

___ The chef looks at his watch and says, "It's time to eat."

___ People hold their stomachs and say they can't eat anymore.

___ The boys and girls carry food to the tables in baskets.

___ People eat and eat and eat.

Word Wheel   Fill in the blanks with words that fit the definitions. The letters of one word are part of the next word.

    1. look at

    2. the state dish of Texas

    3. Ted and Jane's grocery _____

    4. a red light means this

    5. summer is the _____ of winter

    6. a thing, etc.

    7. At a clambake, clams are the _____ food.

    8. Chop the meat _____ small pieces.

    9. small cities

    10. a red, ripe _____ berry

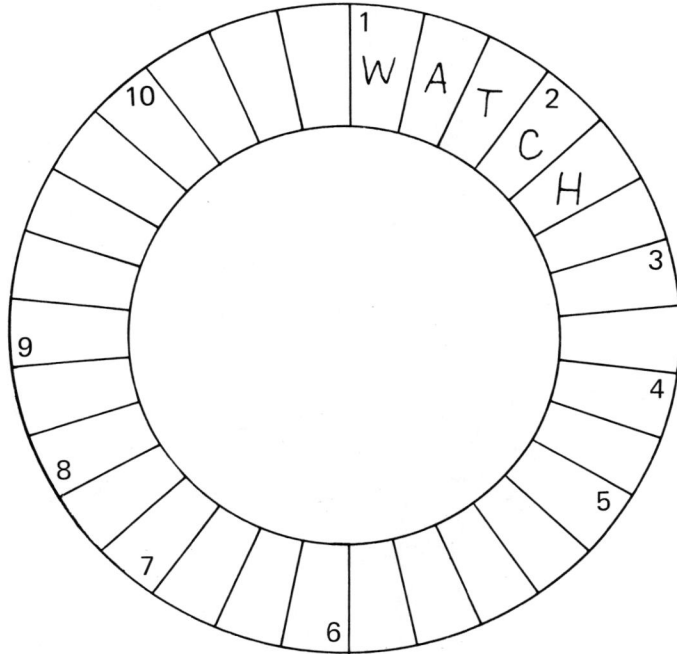

Run for Your Life

PRE-READING

What is happening in the picture?
Is the race beginning or ending?
Describe the people who are running.

READING 1

Scan the passage to find the answers to these questions:

1. How many cigarettes do people in the United States smoke each year?
2. Who is Ted Corbitt?

Read the passage carefully to learn the answer to this question:

Why do many people in the United States run?

¹ Early in the morning, at noon, or in the evening, in big cities and   1
in the countryside, all across the United States, you can see us Americans running. Men and women, children and teenagers, middle-aged people and grandparents are running. People run everywhere—
along the beaches of California, through Central Park in New York,   5
down Main Street in small midwestern towns, around the track, or
at the gymnasium. Some people even run in their living rooms.

² A few years ago, running was not so popular. In the 1960s, runners were mostly athletes and health freaks. In those days, some
people would see a runner and ask, "Hey, what's the hurry?" Or they   10
might say to themselves, "Is he crazy?" Women almost never ran. If
they did, they might hear a man shout, "If I catch you, can I keep
you?" But today all this is changing. Today men and women of all
ages enjoy running.

³ Many of us Americans run for our health. People in the United   15
States smoke about 600 billion cigarettes and drink about 621 million
gallons (2353.6 million l) of wine and liquor each year. Many of us also
like to eat desserts and snack foods. Most of us get too little exercise.
We use our cars instead of our feet. So here we are—a billion pounds
(453.6 million kg) overweight and not very healthy.   20

⁴ Doctors say many of the health problems in the United States
come from these bad habits: eating too much, smoking cigarettes,
and not exercising enough. Doctors tell us, "Eat less, don't smoke,
and exercise more." Running is good exercise because it helps build
a strong heart and lungs. It also helps most people lose weight. One   25
68-year-old grandmother runs 3 times a week. She runs to stay slim.
"I love to eat chocolate sundaes," she says.

⁵ Running is good for health in other ways too. Many runners say

running makes headaches, stomachaches, and other minor medical problems go away. "Running is my doctor," says one man.

⁶ Many runners also enjoy the psychological benefits of running. Ted Corbitt is a famous American runner. He says running helps him relax. Corbitt says, "It's like having your own psychiatrist."

COMPREHENSION CHECK

General Questions   Look at the following statements. Correct them if necessary and add other ideas from the passage.

1. You can see people in the United States running at all times of the day.
2. Runners are mostly young people.
3. Some people run inside.
4. Running was always popular in the United States.
5. Doctors say we need to exercise more and eat less.
6. Running may help headaches go away.

Factual Questions   Answer these questions. You may look back at the passage.

1. Where can you see people running in the United States?
2. Who ran in the 1960s?
3. Who runs now?
4. Why do many Americans run?
5. What bad habits cause our health problems?
6. Why is running a good exercise?
7. Why does the 68-year-old grandmother run?

** Inferential Questions   Answer these questions. Read the passage again if necessary.

1. What do many doctors think of running?
2. Why does one man say, "Running is my doctor"?
3. Why does Corbitt say running is "like having your own psychiatrist"?

What Do You Think?
1. Do most people in your home country run or do other physical exercise? If so, what is the most popular exercise?
2. Do you exercise? Why or why not?
3. Is it good for the 68-year-old grandmother to run three times a week and eat chocolate sundaes?
4. Do you agree that running could make headaches or other minor pains go away? Why or why not?

VOCABULARY SKILLS

Word Search
1. Write the word in line 5 that means *land areas, usually covered with sand, next to water.*

   beaches

2. Write the word in line 9 that means *people who worry too much about their health.*

   health

3. Write the word in line 18 that means *something to eat between meals.*

   snack

4. Write the word in line 25 that means *the organs for breathing.*

   lungs

5. Write the word in line 29 that means *pains in your stomach.*

   stom

6. Write the word in line 31 that means almost the same as *mental and emotional.*

   pys

7. Write the word in line 31 that means *advantages or ways of helping.*

   _____

8. Write the word in line 33 that means *a doctor for mental and emotional problems.*

   psy

Opposites Fill in the blanks with the appropriate word:

(healthy/unhealthy) 1. A few years ago, Sue was not well. She often had headaches and stomachaches. She has a good doctor now and is _healthy_ again.

(less/more) 2. Doctors say we need to eat fewer calories and do _less_ exercise.

(gain/lose) 3. Underweight people need to _____ weight.

(like/dislike) 4. Most Americans don't like walking. They _____ riding in cars instead.

(outside/inside) 5. In good weather, Tim runs in the park, but when it rains, he runs _____.

Word Families running (noun)   *Running* is great exercise.
                                   He put on his *running* shoes.
running (noun-person) Many *runners* like to run outside.
run (verb)   Many Americans *run*.
  ran
  running

Do you want to be a _____? First, buy a good pair of _____ shoes. Next, you'll need some comfortable clothes to _____ in. Now you're ready to begin _____. But don't _____ too much too soon!

smoking (noun)	*Smoking* is bad for your lungs.
	On the airplane he sat in the *"smoking"* section
smoker (noun-person)	He isn't a *smoker*.
smoke (verb)	She likes to *smoke*.
smoked	
smoking	

In 1900, not many women _____ cigarettes. _____ was a male habit. But, today, lots of women _____. In fact, 50 percent of all _____ are women.

READING SKILLS

Scanning

12-Minute Walking/Running Test
Distance (Miles) Covered in 12 Minutes

Fitness category		13-19	20-29	Age (years) 30-39	40-49	50-59	60+
I. Very Poor	(men)	< 1.30*	< 1.22	< 1.18	< 1.14	< 1.03	< .87
	(women)	< 1.0	< .96	< .94	< .88	< .84	< .78
II. Poor	(men)	1.30–1.37	1.22–1.31	1.18–1.30	1.14–1.24	1.03–1.16	.87–1.02
	(women)	1.00–1.18	.96–1.11	.95–1.05	.88– .98	.84– .93	.78– .86
III. Fair	(men)	1.38–1.56	1.32–1.49	1.31–1.45	1.25–1.39	1.17–1.30	1.03–1.20
	(women)	1.19–1.29	1.12–1.22	1.06–1.18	.99–1.11	.94–1.05	.87– .98
IV. Good	(men)	1.57–1.72	1.50–1.64	1.46–1.56	1.40–1.53	1.31–1.44	1.21–1.32
	(women)	1.30–1.43	1.23–1.34	1.19–1.29	1.12–1.24	1.06–1.18	.99–1.09
V. Excellent	(men)	1.73–1.86	1.65–1.76	1.57–1.69	1.54–1.65	1.45–1.58	1.33–1.55
	(women)	1.44–1.51	1.35–1.45	1.30–1.39	1.25–1.34	1.19–1.30	1.10–1.18
VI. Superior	(men)	> 1.87	> 1.77	> 1.70	> 1.66	> 1.59	> 1.56
	(women)	> 1.52	> 1.46	> 1.40	> 1.35	> 1.31	> 1.19

* < Means "less than"; > means "more than."

SOURCE: From *The Aerobics Program for Total Well-Being* by Kenneth H. Cooper. Copyright © 1982 by Kenneth H. Cooper. Reprinted by permission of the publisher, M. Evans and Company, Inc., New York, NY 10017.

Scan the chart on page 222 to answer these questions:

1. You are a 28-year-old woman and can run 1 mile in 12 minutes. What is your fitness category?

   _____

2. You are a 54-year-old man and can run a mile and a quarter in 12 minutes. What is your fitness category?

   _____

3. You want to be in excellent condition, and you are a 35-year-old woman. How many miles would you need to run in 12 minutes?

   _____

4. You are a 42-year-old man and ran a mile and a half in 12 minutes. What is your fitness category?

   _____

5. You are a 59-year-old man. You want to be in excellent condition. How many miles would you need to run in 12 minutes?

   _____

Main Ideas Choose the main idea. The main idea of

1. paragraph 1 is:
   a. Americans run early in the morning.
   b. Some people even run inside.
   c. You can see all types of Americans running everywhere.

2. paragraph 2 is:
   a. Only crazy people ran in the 1960s.
   b. A few years ago, people shouted bad things at runners.
   c. Several years ago, running was not so popular in the United States.

3. paragraph 5 is:
   a. Running can get rid of all your problems.
   b. Running can be better than a doctor.
   c. Running can help minor medical problems.

Read this passage to learn about the Boston Marathon.

The Boston Marathon

Many people run for their health, but others run to win races. The   1
most famous of all races in the United States is the Boston Marathon,
a 26.2-mile (42.2 km) race through part of Boston. The first Boston.
Marathon was in 1897. That year only 15 men ran in the race.

Now about 7000 men and women runners start the race each year.   5
What is the average Boston Marathon runner like? In the 86th Boston Marathon, the average male runner was 37.1 years old, stood 5
feet 9 inches (175.3 cm), and weighed 148.8 pounds (67.5 kg). The
average female was 31.9 years old, stood 5 feet 3 inches (160 cm), and
weighed 114.6 pounds (52 kg).   10

For a long time, this was an all-male race. Roberta Gibb tried to
run in 1966, but she had to hide at the starting line and wait by it
before she could run. Katherine Switzer ran in 1967. She signed her
name on the list of runners as K. V. Switzer. She did not want race
officials to know she was a woman. During the race, officials saw her.   15
They tried to stop her, but she finished the race. In 1972, women
raced in the Marathon officially for the first time. Nina Kurscik won
the women's division that year. She was the mother of three children
and had not started running until her 30s. Miki Gorman came in
second that year. She was 40 and a new mother. In fact, her baby was   20
only 8 months old when Miki ran in the Marathon.

Some runners compete in this race every year. In 1982, John
Kelly, 74, ran in his 51st Boston Marathon. But each year, new runners join the race too. Sister Madonna Bruder, 51, ran her first race
in 1982. She was the first nun to run in the Boston Marathon. She   25
completed the race in 3 hours and 32 minutes, but almost quit during
the last 4 miles (6.4 km). "I had to keep calling on Jesus to keep me
running," she said.

What is it like to run in a marathon? Marathon runner Hal Higdon
says, "The difference between the mile and the marathon is the   30
difference between burning your fingers with a match and being
slowly roasted over hot coals."°

**COMPREHENSION
CHECK**

Answer these questions. You may look back at the passage.

1. What are two reasons to run?
2. How many people ran in the first Boston Marathon?
3. Describe the average Boston Marathon runner.
4. What happened to Katherine Switzer when she ran in 1967?
5. Why was 1972 an important year for women runners?
6. What makes John Kelly unusual?
7. What happened to Sister Bruder during the last part of the Marathon?

READING SKILLS

**Guessing Meanings
from Context**

Choose the best meaning for each italicized word. Use the context to help you.

1. Katherine Switzer ran in 1967. She *signed* her name as K. V. Switzer.
   a. wrote
   b. said
   c. changed

2. During the race, officials saw her. They tried to stop her, but she finished the race. In 1972, women raced in the Marathon *officially* for the first time.
   a. slowly
   b. carefully
   c. legally, openly

3. In 1972, women raced in the Marathon officially for the first time. Nina Kurscik won the women's *division* that year.
   a. part of the race
   b. money
   c. prize

4. The difference between the mile and the marathon is the difference between burning your fingers with a match and being slowly *roasted* over hot *coals*.

Roasted over hot coals

Roasted means:	*Coals* are:
a. fed	a. fuel for fire
b. cooked over a fire	b. food
c. moved	c. feet

Connections Connect the underlined words to the words they refer to. Refer to the example on page 85 if necessary.

1. In the 1960s, runners were mostly athletes and health freaks. <u>In those days,</u> some people would see a runner and ask, "Hey, what's the hurry?"

2. Doctors say many of the health problems in the United States came from <u>these bad habits:</u> smoking cigarettes, eating too much, and not exercising enough.

3. He says running helps him relax. Corbitt says, "<u>It</u>'s like having your own psychiatrist."

4. In 1972, women raced in the Marathon officially for the first time. Nina Kurscik won the women's division <u>that year.</u>

5. Some runners compete in <u>this race</u> every year. In 1982, John Kelly, 74, ran in his 51st Boston Marathon.

**Analogies   An analogy is a comparison.

Examples

1. She thinks *like* a fox.
2. He eats *like* a horse.

Study the analogy in line 33 in Reading 1 and fill in the blanks:

1. For Ted Corbitt, running is like having

_____

Explain what Corbitt means:

_____

_____

_____

Now study the analogy in lines 30–33 in Reading 2 and fill in the blanks:

2. For Higdon, running a mile is like burning your fingers and running a marathon is like

_____ _____

Explain what Higdon means:

_____

_____

_____

We can also make analogies in another way. Look at these examples:

1. That man *is a fox.* = That man *is like a fox.*
2. He *is a piece of ice.* = He *is like a piece of ice.*

Now study the analogy in line 30 of Reading 1 and fill in the blanks:

One man says that running is

_____

Explain what he means:

_____

_____

_____

CHAPTER REVIEW

1. List reasons Americans run:

   _____

   _____

   _____

   _____

2. Tell about Sister Madonna Bruder:

   _____

   _____

   _____

   _____

POST-READING ACTIVITY

Word Find There are more than 25 words with two or more letters in this puzzle. Move one letter at a time in any direction: up, down, horizontally, or diagonally to make words. Don't jump or skip letters.

T H E   *the*

I R A   *there*

E D S   _____

N O T   _____

_____

_____

_____

_____

_____

_____

_____

_____

_____

_____

_____

_____

_____

_____

_____

_____

_____

_____

_____

_____

16

Modern Nomads

PRE-READING

Describe the picture.

What kind of people own trailers?

Why do they own trailers?

What is the connection between the picture and the title?

READING 1

Scan the passage to learn the answers to these questions:

1. What is the name of the travel club?
2. How many people belong to this club?

Read the passage carefully to learn the answers to these questions:

1. What kinds of people join this club?
2. Why do they join this club?

> A restless man is the nomad,
> Traveling from place to place.
> Always looking, never finding
> A place to rest his head.

¹ From Guadalajara, Mexico, to Nova Scotia, Canada, on big super-highways and small country roads, you can see cars pulling long, silver trailers. You can find these trailers and their owners in major parks and campgrounds. Who are these people and where are they going?

² These people with their aluminum houses on wheels are the modern nomads of the United States. Many of them belong to a large travel club, the Wally Byam Caravan Club International. For them, travel is a way of life.

³ About 26,000 people belong to this caravan club. Some of the people are full-time members, usually older, retired people, like Bea and Andy Kaiser. The Kaisers do not own a house. They live in their trailer and travel with it all year. Other people in the club are part-time members, usually younger people with families. Most of them only travel in the summer or during other long vacations.

⁴ Members of the club pay a yearly fee. For this fee, they get a directory with the names and trailer numbers of all the club members. They also get a monthly travel magazine. The magazine lists all the monthly parties, meetings, or activities in the United States, Mexico, and Canada.

⁵ People join the caravan club for other reasons than getting the directory or magazine. Some people join because caravanning is an easy and inexpensive way to travel. However, most of the members —older, retired people—join the caravan club to escape or get away from some of the economic, social, and psychological problems of retirement.

⁶ Retired club members have fewer economic or money worries than other retired people. A trailer costs much less than a house, so there are no expensive payments to worry about. A trailer is also much smaller than a house, so there are fewer household items, such ₃₀ as furniture, to worry about.

⁷ These people also escape many of the social and psychological problems of retirement. There are always places to go, things to see, and different activities to participate in. With 26,000 club members, there are many chances to meet new people. As one member said, ₃₅ "I call it a way of staying alive."

⁸ Now, however, fewer people are joining the club. Because of inflation, the cost of a trailer and the cost of gasoline are greater. However, you can still find people traveling on big highways and little country roads going somewhere. ₄₀

COMPREHENSION CHECK

General Questions   Look at the following statements: Correct them if necessary and add other ideas from the passage.

1. Many people with trailers belong to the caravan club.
2. Only retired people belong to the Wally Byam Club.
3. The Wally Byam Club is free.
4. People join the club because it's a good way to travel.
5. Young people join to escape problems.
6. Fewer people are joining the caravan club now than before.

Factual Questions   Answer these questions. You may look back at the passage.

1. What kind of people are full-time members?
2. When do part-time members travel?
3. What do people get in return for their yearly fee?
4. What are some reasons for joining the club?
5. What does the club magazine contain?
6. Why do retired members have fewer money worries?
7. How do club members escape the social problems of retirement?

✳✳ Inferential Questions   Answer these questions. Read the passage again if necessary.

1. What are nomads?
2. How do club members feel about travel?
3. Why do full-time members live in their trailers?
4. Why don't part-time members travel all the time?
5. How do members learn about parties or meetings?
6. Why would a directory be helpful?
7. Why is a trailer more economical than a house?

What Do You Think?

1. Does your country have nomads? If yes, how are they different from the Wally Byam nomads?
2. How do retired people live in your country? Alone? With their children? In special institutions?
3. What problems do retired people usually have? Do the retired people in your country have the same problems as people in the U.S.?
4. How much independence do elderly people in your country have?
5. What will you do when you retire? Where will you live? How will you spend your time?

VOCABULARY SKILLS

Word Search

1. Write the word in the poem that means *always moving around.*

   _____

2. Write the word in line 8 that means *a group of people traveling together.*

   _____

3. Write the word in line 11 that means *people belonging to an organization.*

   _____

4. Write the word in line 17 that means *a book listing names and telephone numbers.*

   _____

5. Write the word in line 29 that means *think constantly about problems.*

   _____

6. Write the word in line 30 that means *belonging to a house.*

_____

Word Usage   Look at this example:

    yearly = once a year

Fill in the meanings of these words:

monthly = _____

weekly = _____

daily = _____

Use the listed words to fill in the blanks:

1. Most newspapers are _____ papers.
2. *National Geographic* has 12 magazines a year. It is a

    _____ magazine.
3. *Time* has 52 issues a year. It is a _____ magazine.
4. You should practice English _____.
5. Independence Day is a _____ celebration.
6. Someone cleans the classroom every day. It is cleaned

    _____.

Idioms and Expressions   *belong to* = be a member of

Look at this example:

    Bea and Andy Kaiser *belong to* this club. $=$ Bea and Andy Kaiser are *members of* this club.

Answer these questions:

1. What kind of people belong to the Wally Byam Caravan Club International?
2. Why do they belong to this club?
3. What clubs do you belong to?

belong to = **be owned by**

Look at this example:

The trailer *belongs to* the Kaisers. } = { The trailer is owned by the Kaisers.

Use objects from the classroom to make questions like these:

1. Who does this notebook belong to? It belongs to Mary.
2. Who does this sweater belong to? It belongs to Joe.

Word Families

psychology (noun)
psychologist (noun-person)
psychological (adjective)

Sue wants to major in *psychology.*
She wants to be a child *psychologist.*
She is interested in the *psychological* problems of children.

Use the listed words to fill in the blanks:

Dr. Carpenter is a _____. He has a degree in _____ from New York University. His area of interest is the _____ of older people. He is interested in the _____ problems of retired people. His daughter, Sue, is also interested in _____. But she is more interested in the _____ of children.

READING SKILLS

Guessing Meanings from Context

Choose the best meaning for each italicized word. Use the context to help you.

1. "A restless man is the *nomad*, traveling from place to place."
   a. person traveling on vacation
   b. traveling salesman
   c. person moving constantly

2. Members of this club pay a yearly *fee.*
   a. money
   b. payment
   c. change

3. There are fewer *household items,* such as furniture, to worry about.
   a. things belonging in a house
   b. things taken to a house
   c. things put in a house to be safe

4. Because of *inflation,* the cost of a trailer and the cost of gasoline are greater.
   a. increased volumes
   b. increased sizes
   c. increased prices

Sentence Splitting   Look at this example:

These people own trailers, aluminum houses on wheels.

The sentence contains two sentences:

1. These people own trailers.
2. The trailers are aluminum houses on wheels.

Split the following sentences:

A. They belong to a large travel club, the Wally Byam Caravan Club International.

   1. _____

   2. _____

B. Some of the people are full-time members, usually older, retired people, like Bea and Andy Kaiser.

   1. _____

   2. _____

C. Other people in the club are part-time members, usually younger people with families.

   1. _____

   2. _____

D. Most of the members—old, retired people—join the caravan club to escape retirement problems.

1. _____

2. _____

Main Ideas   Choose the main idea. The main idea of

1. paragraph 1 is:
   a. People travel in the United States.
   b. You can find people with trailers everywhere.
   c. People have long, silver trailers.

2. paragraph 3 is:
   a. Members of the caravan are full-time or part-time.
   b. There are 26,000 people in the caravan club.
   c. Bea and Andy Kaiser are retired.

3. paragraph 5 is:
   a. People join to get the directory and the magazine.
   b. Older, retired people join the club.
   c. People join the caravan club for different reasons.

4. paragraph 7 is:
   a. People join the club to escape their problems.
   b. Everyone joins to meet new people.
   c. Retired people join to escape problems of retirement.

5. the whole passage is:
   a. The caravan club is a way of life for some people.
   b. People with trailers join a caravan club.
   c. Nomads belong to the caravan club.

READING 2   Read the passage to learn the answer to this question:

What was the annual meeting like?

Wally Byam caravanners travel all over North and Central Amer-   1
ica to attend the 1300 yearly parties, meetings, or activities. Caravanners can attend the fall caravan in Bangor, Maine, or the National
Orange Show in San Bernardino, California. Those interested in
fishing can attend the Nova Scotia Fishing Reunion in Lunenber,   5

Nova Scotia. For others, there is a 35-day caravan tour through Mexico or a 45-day tour through eastern Canada.

One of the most important events in the year is the annual meeting. In 1981, Andy Kaiser, club president at that time, was responsible for planning the event. About 3000 club members got together   10
in Ames, Iowa, for the 24th annual meeting. More than 2000 shiny, aluminum trailers parked in grassy fields and empty parking lots under the hot July sun.

The meeting was like a little community on wheels. Some members bought stamps and mailed letters at the club's own post office   15
trailer, and others made telephone calls at the club's own telephone trailer. Their own band played, and their own chorus sang.

A nearby building served as the central meeting place. There were bulletin boards and sign-up tables. The bulletin boards listed information about the daily activities, birthdays and anniversaries of   20
the day, and even some items for sale. Club members signed up for tours of the area and for committee work. They signed up for the parking committee, the welcoming committee, or the games committee. Members of the maintenance committee kept the meeting area clean.   25

There were also many different kinds of activities to sign up for. There were bingo games and bridge games. There was an early morning walkers group, and an early morning exercise group. Members could also sign up for the fashion show and see the newest fashions.   30

Around the sign-up tables, different caravan groups had displays of their own state activities. The Oklahoma group advertised its Oklahoma breakfast, and the Washington group gave information about its salmon fishing meeting in Lacey, Washington.

Everyone was busy that week. They participated in the activities,   35
sang and danced, visited with old friends, and made new ones. At the end of the week, they went in all directions—perhaps to meet again in New York, Colorado, New Mexico, or British Columbia.

**COMPREHENSION
CHECK**

Answer these questions. You may look back at the passage.

1. Where can caravanners attend the 1300 club activities?
2. What do caravanners in Lunenber, Nova Scotia do?

3. What tours can caravanners attend?
4. Who was responsible for planning the 1981 annual meeting?
5. Why was the meeting like a little community on wheels?
6. Where did caravanners get information?
7. Where did the caravanners go at the end of the week?

Idioms and Expressions *sign* = write your name, write your official signature

Examples

1. *Sign* your name at the bottom.
2. This paper isn't official. You didn't *sign* your name.

sign up = register

Examples

1. I want to *sign up* for a course in Mexican cooking.
2. Before you go on the trip, you have to *sign up*.

Use *sign* or *sign up* in the blanks:

1. He will _____ his name with an "X."

2. _____ on the bottom line.

3. Mary wanted to _____ for the tennis competition.

4. Please, _____ this piece of paper.

5. Here is the list for you to _____ on.

** Vocabulary in Context

anniversary	committees	reunion
activities	display	signs up
annual	list	

Choose from the listed words and fill in the blanks:

Today is my grandparents' 75th wedding _____. For the last ten years, their anniversary has been a big family _____ where everyone gets together. It's an _____ event that everyone wants to attend. Months before, my uncle organizes several _____ to take care of the different _____. Each family _____ for a different event. Several families volunteer to bring the food. One family volunteers to write out the guest _____ and the invitations. Another family takes care of a _____ of family photographs. There is always a lot of preparation, but everyone has a wonderful time.

READING SKILLS

Guessing Meanings from Context

Choose the best meaning of each italicized word. Use the context to help you.

1. Their own *chorus* sang.
   a. group of singers
   b. group of dancers
   c. group of musicians

2. The *bulletin board* listed information about the activities of the day.
   a. piece of wood
   b. place for coats
   c. place for special notices

3. Members of the *maintenance committee* kept the meeting area clean.
   a. committee for cleaning and repair
   b. committee for clean main events
   c. committee for clean meetings

4. The Washington group gave information to fishermen about its *salmon* meeting in Lacey, Washington.
   a. kind of reunion
   b. kind of color
   c. kind of fish

5. Members could also sign up for the *fashion show* and see members wearing the newest fashions.
   a. display of methods
   b. display of clothes
   c. display of sewing

Connections   Connect the underlined words or groups of words to the idea they refer to. Refer to the example on page 85 if necessary.

1. Caravanners can attend the fall caravan in Bangor, Maine. <u>Those</u> interested in fishing can attend the Nova Scotia fishing reunion. For <u>others,</u> there are tours through Mexico or eastern Canada.

2. In 1981, Andy Kaiser, club president <u>at that time,</u> was responsible for planning the event.

3. Some members bought stamps and mailed letters at their own post office trailer, and <u>others</u> made phone calls at the club's own telephone trailer.

4. They participated in the activities, sang and danced, visited with old friends, and made new <u>ones.</u>

Scanning   Scan the announcement on page 243 to answer the following questions:

1. When is the fishing derby?
2. Where is the meeting?
3. When do tours begin?
4. Where will members fish?
5. Who will play for the dancers?
6. What kind of activities will there be?

**August 9-16
Fishing Derby**

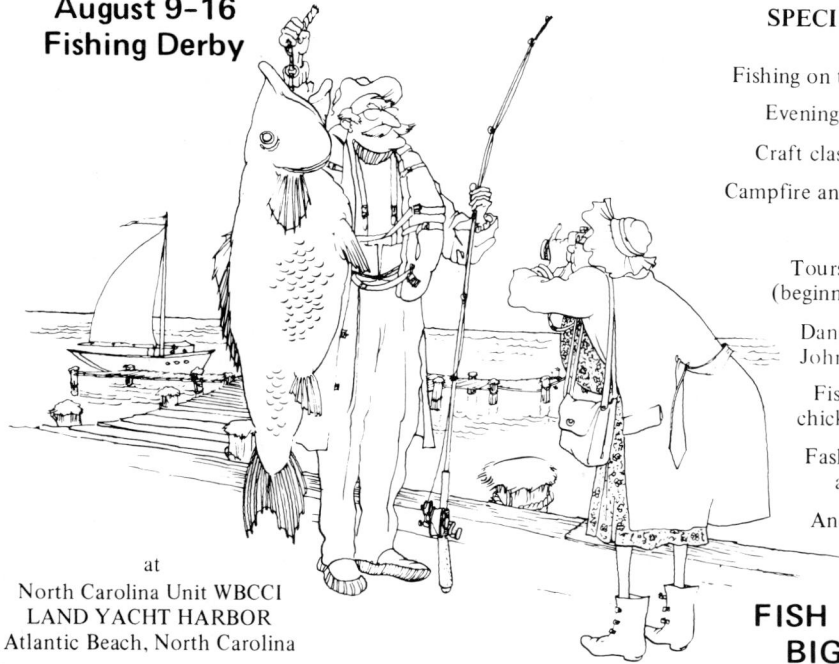

at
North Carolina Unit WBCCI
LAND YACHT HARBOR
Atlantic Beach, North Carolina

SPECIAL EVENTS

Fishing on the Atlantic Ocean

Evening entertainment

Craft classes and displays

Campfire and cookout program

Games

Tours of the area
(beginning August 5)

Dancing with the
John Beard Band

Fish fry and
chicken dinners

Fashion show
and tea

And more —

**FISH FOR THE
BIG ONES**

CHAPTER REVIEW

1. Give reasons for joining the Wally Byam Caravan Club International:

_____

_____

_____

_____

2. Describe activities of the club.

_____

_____

_____

3. Describe the 24th annual meeting.

_____

_____

_____

_____

**POST-READING
ACTIVITY**

Logic Problem   Read the information to find the answer to the question: Who has the monkey? As you read the information, fill in the boxes on the chart.

There are five trailers in the campground.
Each trailer has a flag of a different color.
People from five different states live in the trailers.
The people in each trailer are going to different places.
They drive different cars.
They keep different pets.

1. The people from Virginia are in the middle trailer.
2. The people with the snake are in the trailer on the far right.
3. The people who are going to Dallas are in the trailer next to the one with the red flag.
4. The people in the trailer to the left of the one with the green flag drive a Mercedes.
5. The people who live in the trailer with the blue flag are going to Disneyland.
6. The people from California are in the trailer next to the people going to Dallas.
7. The people with the poodle live next to the people going to Disneyland.
8. The people from Virginia drive a van.
9. The people in the second trailer from the left are from Florida.
10. The people who have a cat are from South Dakota.
11. The people from Oregon drive a Land Rover.
12. The people from Florida live next to the people with a parrot.
13. The people in the trailer with the orange flag are going to New Orleans.
14. The people who drive a station wagon live next to the people going to the Rocky Mountains.
15. The people going to Washington, D.C., drive a truck.

	🚩 RED	🚩 YELLOW	🚩 GREEN	🚩 BLUE	🚩 ORANGE
STATE	california	Florida	VIRGINIA (7)	south dakota	oregan
DESTINATION	washington DC	dallas	Rocky mts	dismeyland	new orleans
VEHICLE	truck	mercedes	van	station wagon	land rover
PET	parrot		poodle	cat	snake

Community
Theater

17

PRE-READING

Describe the picture.

Do you think the theater is a professional one? Why or why not?

READING 1

Scan the passage to find the answers to these questions:

1. When did Henry Fonda first start acting?
2. When did community theaters first appear?
3. What is ACTA?

Now read the passage carefully to learn the answer to this question:

What is the purpose of community theaters?

[1] A community theater is an important part of almost every city or town in the United States. There are over 2000 community theaters in the United States today. About 4.5 million people work or perform in these theaters for an audience of more than 50 million people annually.

[2] These theaters are amateur organizations and are different from professional theater companies. A community theater may have its own building or perform in a school or church auditorium. The actors and actresses do not receive money for their work in the community theater. They have other jobs to support themselves instead. Small communities cannot support a full-time theater. They cannot pay actors, directors, or stage workers, so the theater participants work for free.

[3] A community theater may be called amateur because the actors do not get money, but its performances can be almost professional. Because of their professional performances, some community theaters are asked to perform in other countries. Theater Memphis in Tennessee performed in Austria, and the Omaha Community Playhouse in Nebraska performed in Bulgaria.

[4] Many professional actors and actresses began acting in community theaters. One famous American actor, Henry Fonda, first began acting in the Omaha Community Playhouse in 1925. In 1928, he went to New York and later became a famous movie star.

[5] Community theaters first appeared after World War I. Before the war, communities had no need for their own theaters because professional theater companies called road shows would travel around the country. Each road show with famous actors or actresses performed only once in each community and then returned the next year with a new show.

[6] The road shows almost disappeared around 1914 because of the high cost of railroad transportation. Actors and stage workers demanded higher wages, but the road shows had no money to give them. Then, during the war, there were even fewer road shows because of economic conditions and the competition from movies.

[7] After World War I, people in big cities saw plays, but most people in smaller towns did not. Small groups of people thought their communities should be able to see plays, so they got together to organize drama groups. Performing plays was, and still is, one of the main purposes of community theaters.

[8] Another purpose of community theater is to provide an opportunity for creative work. Many people join community theaters because they want to perform or to be creative. Several people in a community theater group were asked why they joined. Each one said he or she needed to be creative—to do something original. One man said, "I love to act. It's the only time I feel alive." Another said, "I have a very boring job. In a play, I can create something." One woman said, "My whole life is occupied with husband and family. I need something more than that."

[9] The third purpose of community theater is to educate and improve the community. Theater is an art, but it also introduces new ideas to the audience.

[10] Richard Fliehr is a doctor and the president of ACTA, American Community Theater Association. He said the responsibility of a community theater is "to educate its audience in all forms of drama." When he spoke to the members of the theater organization he said, "You must produce not only quality in your theater; you must improve the quality of life in your community."

COMPREHENSION CHECK

General Questions   Look at the following statements. Correct them if necessary and add other ideas from the passage.

1. A community theater is an amateur organization.
2. Community theaters never travel outside of the United States.
3. All movie actors begin their careers in community theaters.

4. Many road shows traveled around the country during World War I.
5. Community theater gives people the chance to be creative.

Factual Questions   Answer these questions. You may look back at the passage.

1. Do the actors and actresses in community theaters get paid?
2. Where do some professional actors and actresses begin their careers?
3. Who was Henry Fonda?
4. Where did road shows travel?
5. How often did the road shows perform in each community?
6. Why did road shows disappear?
7. How did small towns provide drama for their communities?
8. Why do people join community theaters?
9. What are the three main purposes of community theaters?
10. What does Richard Fliehr think is the responsibility of community theaters?

✱✱ Inferential Questions   Answer these questions. Read the passage again if necessary.

1. How do the actors and actresses in community theaters support themselves?
2. Where can a future actor or stage worker get good experience?
3. Could any community theater travel to another country?
4. How did road shows travel?
5. Why was most theater activity located in big cities after the war?
6. What can theater do for a community?

What Do You Think?   1. Did you ever participate in a play? If yes, when? What did you do?
2. Are there any amateur theater groups where you live? If yes, are they popular? Why or why not?
3. Would you like to be a part of a community theater? If no, why not? If yes, what would you like to do? Act? Make costumes? Work on the stage?
4. Do you think people have a need to be creative? In what ways can this need be expressed?

VOCABULARY SKILLS

Word Search

1. Write the word in line 4 that means *to act.*

   perform

2. Write the word in line 4 that means *people watching a play.*

   audience

3. Write the word in line 8 that means a *room where an audience sits.*

   auditorium

4. Write the word in line 24 that means *came into sight.* bên thấy

   appeared

5. Write the word in lines 31–32 that means *asked for.*

   demade

6. Write the word in line 40 that means *to make available.*

   _____

7. Write the word in line 46 that means *to make something new.*

   _____

8. Write the word in line 56 that means *a high degree of goodness.*

   _____

Opposites

We can make some words have the opposite meaning by adding the prefix *dis-*. Choose from the listed pairs of words to fill in the blanks.

(like / dislike)

1. Many people spend their free time watching TV, but I don't. I _____ to read instead.

(appeared / disappeared)

2. We watched as the plane took off, climbed into the sky, and _____.

(continue / discontinue)

3. It's only November, and the weather is already cold. I guess the cold weather will _____ for three or four months.

(agree/disagree)

4. Quinn thinks they should paint the house green, but his wife doesn't _____ with him. She prefers gray.

(connected/disconnected)

5. Operator, can you help me? I was calling my family long-distance in California, and we were _____.

Word Families   performance (noun)

Did you see Henry Fonda's *performance* in "On Golden Pond"?

performer (noun-person)
perform (verb)
  performed
  performing

The *performers* wore bright costumes. The Omaha Community Playhouse will *perform* four plays this year.

Use the listed words to fill in the blanks:

Our high school is preparing for their first musical show this year. They plan to _____ "Oklahoma." They will _____ every Friday and Saturday night for three weeks. There will be a total of six _____. The musical has only six major characters, but there will be a lot of other _____ singing and dancing. We hope you can come to one of our _____.

READING SKILLS

Guessing Meanings from Context

Choose the best meaning for each italicized word. Use the context to help you.

1. Small communities cannot *support* a full-time theater. They cannot pay actors, directors, or stage workers.
   a. provide help for
   b. provide money for
   c. provide an audience for

2. Before World War I, certain theater groups called *road shows* would travel around the country.
   a. traveling amateur actors
   b. traveling communities
   c. traveling theater companies

3. Actors and stage workers demanded higher *wages*, but the road shows had no more money to give them.
   a. pay
   b. increases
   c. costs

Main Ideas   Choose the main idea. The main idea of

1. paragraph 2 is:
   a. Community theaters sometimes use churches or schools.
   b. Everyone works full-time.
   c. The people in community theaters are volunteers.

2. paragraph 5 is:
   a. Professional theater companies were called road shows.
   b. Before the war communities had road shows and so didn't need their own theaters.
   c. Famous actors and actresses performed in road shows.

3. paragraph 7 is:
   a. Only the people in big cities saw plays.
   b. People mainly wanted to see live theater and road shows.
   c. People organized theater groups to bring drama to their towns.

4. paragraph 8 is:
   a. People join community theaters because they want to act.
   b. Community theaters provide a chance for creativity.
   c. One man said he had a boring job.

5. paragraph 10 is:
   a. Community theater should improve people's lives.
   b. Community theater has three main purposes.
   c. Richard Fliehr is a doctor and president of ACTA.

READING 2

Jennifer is the director of a community theater in a small town. This is her letter to Richard, the former director. Read the letter carefully to learn the answer to this question:

What problems does Jennifer have?

April 15th 1

Dear Richard,

I give up! The whole thing is useless and stupid. I'm so angry! Why did I ever volunteer for this job as director? Nothing at the dress rehearsal went right. What can I do? There is only one more month 5
of practice before we open.

Everything went wrong. First of all, our main actor, Bill, was sick and couldn't come. His mother said he had a bad cold. How can we have a good opening night when the star actor is coughing and sneezing all over the stage? 10

That wasn't all. We were waiting for Act 1 to begin, but the curtain wouldn't open. Last week, it wouldn't close, and today it wouldn't open. It took Joe, the stage worker, 30 minutes to fix that curtain.

Then we started Act 1. Suddenly the lights in the auditorium went out. It was so dark we couldn't see a thing. Sam got frightened, fell 15
over a chair, and cut his leg a little. All of this happened in 3 minutes of darkness. Then it took Sam 20 minutes to go to the dressing room, put a Band-Aid on the cut, and change his torn pants. Joe checked the lights, but nothing was wrong. How strange! By the time Sam got back, the other actors were restless. Luckily, there were no more 20
problems, so we could finish with Act 1.

Without taking a break, we started Act 2. In the middle of the act, everything stopped because Maria didn't come on stage. Where was Maria? She was behind the door trying to open it. She said the door was locked. Locked? That door didn't even have a lock! Joe had to go 25
and fix that too, and then we were able to finish rehearsing Act 2.

But my problems weren't over—not yet. There was worse to come. In Act 3, Maria had a big argument with her boyfriend. After a lot of shouting, Maria was supposed to go out the door and slam it

behind her with a bang. That stupid door wouldn't close. In Act 2, 30
the door wouldn't open, and now it wouldn't close. I was beginning
to get angry. I told Joe to fix it again, and I told Maria to slam the door
very hard.

Then, Maria and her boyfriend started their argument again.
Maria opened the door, walked out of the room, and slammed the 35
door behind her.

Well, you just wouldn't believe what happened. All the walls on
the stage fell down! And there was that door still standing open. I was
so angry I told everyone to go home. We turned off the lights, and
left the auditorium. That door was the only thing standing on the 40
stage.

Was it this bad when you were director?

Jennifer

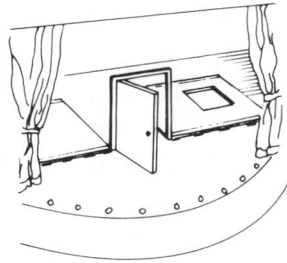

COMPREHENSION CHECK

Answer these questions. You may look back at the passage.

1. Who was writing about the dress rehearsal?
2. Why didn't Bill come to the rehearsal?
3. What was wrong with the curtain?
4. What was wrong with the lights?
5. Was Sam badly hurt?
6. Why didn't Maria come on stage?
7. Why did everyone go home?
8. Why does Jennifer want to give up being a director?

VOCABULARY SKILLS

∗∗ Vocabulary in Context

curtains   professional
director   provided
dressing rooms   rehearsals
performed   stage

Choose from the listed words and fill in the blanks:

I remember my high school drama-club days. We _____ several plays each year. One of the English teachers was our _____. She chose the plays and the actors, and told us what to do. _____ were always after school, and the final dress rehearsals were usually at night.

I mostly worked as a stage manager. My job was to open and close the _____, to put the furniture on the _____, and to help the actors dress. Of course, we didn't have any _____ to change our clothes in. We just used a classroom near the school auditorium.

Our performances were never very _____. We made many mistakes on and behind the stage. Everyone, however, had a good time, and we _____ some fun for our classmates and our families.

READING SKILLS

Guessing Meanings from Context

Choose the best meaning for each italicized word. Use the context to help you.

1. Nothing at the dress *rehearsal* went right. There is only one more night of practice before we open.
   a. practice for a play
   b. practice dressing
   c. practice to be first

2. Sam went to the *dressing room* and changed his torn pants.
   a. room for dresses
   b. room for changing clothes
   c. room for first aid

3. Sam put a *Band-Aid* on the cut on his leg.
   a. something to cover an injury
   b. something to keep things together
   c. something to help you dance.

4. Maria had a big *argument* with her boyfriend. After a lot of shouting, Maria went out the door.
   a. happy conversation
   b. sad discussion
   c. disagreement

5. Maria was supposed to go out the door and *slam* it hard behind her with a bang.
   a. hit
   b. close
   c. knock

CHAPTER REVIEW

1. Describe the purposes of community theater:

   _____

   _____

   _____

   _____

2. Give the history of community theaters.

   _____

   _____

   _____

   _____

   _____

POST-READING ACTIVITY

Fill-in Puzzle   All the words for the puzzle are connected with the theater. The words are in alphabetical order and are grouped by the number of letters in each word. Put the words into the correct places in the puzzle.

2 letters

at (a show)
to (the theater)

3 letters

act
put (on a play)

4 letters

acts
cost (of the tickets)
live (theater)
play
rest (between acts)
seat
show

5 letters

actor
dress

6 letters

lights

7 letters

actress
costume
curtain
perform
theater
tickets

8 letters

amateurs
audience

9 letters

performer
rehearsal

10 letters

auditorium

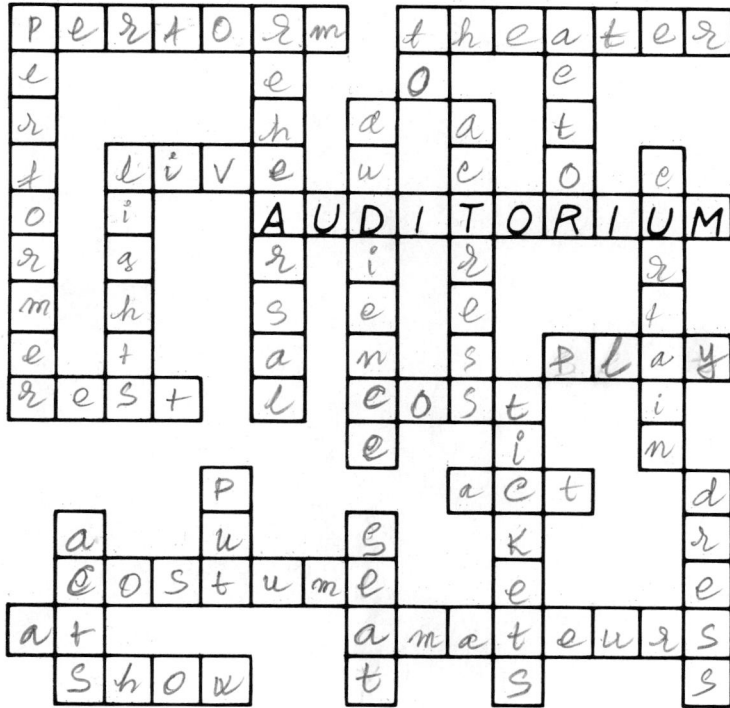

PERFORM THEATER

performer
rehearsal
platform
live
auditorium
AUDITORIUM
rehearsal
audience
costume
rest
PLAY
act
painting
costume
at amateurs
show

Rodeo

cuộc đấu bò ở dua gga

PRE-READING

Describe the picture.
Where is the action probably taking place?
What is a rodeo?

261

READING 1

Scan the passage to find the answers to these questions:

1. How much does the bucking bull weigh?
2. How much money did Paul Tierney make in 1980?

Now read the passage carefully to learn the answers to these questions:

1. What happens at a typical rodeo?
2. Why do cowboys take part in rodeos?

1 The noisy rodeo crowd suddenly becomes quiet, the gray, 1
wooden gate swings open, and we see our first cowboy. He is a tall,
thin man in his early 20s. He is riding a wild, bucking 1500-pound
(779.5 kg) bull. He stays on the animal's back for just 7 seconds before
it bucks him off, and he lands on the ground of the dusty arena. The 5
crowd grows excited. For a moment, the cowboy lies on the ground,
and the angry animal moves toward him. A rodeo clown runs up to
the bull and waves a large, red handkerchief. He wants to get the
animal's attention. The bull notices the colorful clown and starts
toward him. At the same time, the cowboy jumps up, dusts off his 10
jeans, and runs out of the arena. He will be back later. Now it is time
for another cowboy to try his luck with a bucking bull.

2 The longer the cowboy stays on, the more prize money he wins.
A good rider will stay on a bull for about 8 seconds before it bucks
him off and he lands on the ground. (Cowboys call this "getting 15
dusted.")

3 Bull riding is one of the most exciting and dangerous parts of the
rodeo, but there is also calf roping, cattle wrestling, barrel° racing,
and many other events. Calf ropers try to put a rope around a calf
and tie its legs together as fast as they can. Cattle wrestlers try to 20
throw a steer to the ground. Barrel racers ride their horses through
rows of barrels. Rodeo clowns make the crowd laugh, but they also
help save the lives of cowboys. When a bull moves toward a fallen
rider, the clown moves in to get the animal's attention.

4 Rodeos are fun, but they are serious business for the competitors. 25
A few cowboys make lots of money in rodeos. In 1980, the top prize
winner was Paul Tierney. He won about $105,000 in prize money.

5 Some cowboys make lots of money, but they do not have easy

Barrel

lives. A cowboy who wants to make as much money as Paul Tierney has to work hard. He has to take part in at least 100 rodeos a year. That means he often enters 2 or 3 rodeos in one weekend. He may be in one rodeo event in Wyoming on Friday afternoon, and another one in Montana on Saturday morning. How does he get around so fast? The top cowboys usually have their own planes to help them get from one rodeo to another quickly, but the typical rodeo competitors drive their trucks thousands of miles month after month.

⁶ Of course, competing in rodeos is also dangerous. Don Gay is one of the lucky cowboys. He says he has never been seriously injured. But one time a bull threw his horns under Gay's left arm. The doctors sewed Gay up with 63 stitches. Ten days later, Gay rode in the National Finals Rodeo and tore most of the stitches in another accident. But Gay is still lucky. Each year, several cowboys die while competing in rodeos.

⁷ So why do cowboys take part in rodeos? Mike Waters, a former International Rodeo Association World Champion Cowboy, says he does not want to live a dull, ordinary life. He does not want to work from 8 to 5, read a newspaper, and go to bed. He likes to travel, and he likes the rodeo people he works with. Other people say they compete in rodeos mainly for the money. For these people, riding in rodeos is just a way to make a living. Says one such cowboy, "I don't consider it a big deal; some people play golf, some people fly. Why not ride in a rodeo?"

COMPREHENSION CHECK

General Questions   Look at the following statements. Correct them if necessary and add other ideas from the passage.

1. The first cowboy is young.
2. The clown runs away from the bull.
3. A good rider will stay on the bull for less than two seconds.
4. Today, some cowboys make a lot of money in rodeos.
5. Competing in rodeos is dangerous.
6. Cowboy Mike Waters just wants an ordinary life.

Factual Questions   Answer these questions. You may look back at the passage.

1. What happens when the gate swings open?
2. What happens when the bull sees the clown?
3. What is one of the most dangerous and exciting parts of the rodeo?
4. What do calf ropers do?
5. What do barrel racers do?
6. How far do the typical rodeo competitors drive their trucks?
7. What happened to cowboy Don Gay?

✲✲ Inferential Questions   Answer these questions. Read the passage again if necessary.

1. Why does the crowd become quiet?
2. Why do cowboys call falling off an animal "getting dusted"?
3. Why is bull riding exciting and dangerous?
4. How many rodeos does a top cowboy take part in?
5. How can cowboys take part in 2 or 3 rodeos in one weekend?
6. Why is Don Gay lucky?

What Do You Think?   1. Did you ever want to be a cowboy or cowgirl when you were a child? Why or why not?
2. What would you like or dislike most about the life of a cowboy or cowgirl? Why?
3. What events in your country are similar to the rodeo?
4. Why do you think rodeos are so popular in North America?
5. Are rodeos or similar events popular in your country? Why or why not?

VOCABULARY SKILLS

Word Search   1. Write the word in line 2 that means *an opening in a wall or fence.*

_____gate_____

2. Write the word in line 3 that means *jumping up with four feet together and the back arched.*

_____bucking_____

3. Write the word in line 5 that means *a place where a contest or competition takes place.*

_____arena_____

4. Write the word in line 18 that means *a young bull or cow.*

   cattle

5. Write the word in line 18 that means *throwing a person or animal to the ground.*

   wrestling

6. Write the word in line 46 that means *the opposite of exciting.*

   dull

7. Write the word in line 49 that means almost the same as *mostly.*

   mainly

Opposites   Use the appropriate word in each blank:

	The little girl said she wanted to be a
(cowgirl/cowboy)	_____. Her brother wanted to be
(cowgirl/cowboy)	a _____. "Rodeos might seem
(dull/exciting)	_____," their uncle said, "but
(safe/dangerous)	they are also _____. You can
(win/lose)	_____ a lot of money, but you can
(win/lose)	_____ your life." The children said
(safe/dangerous)	they knew rodeos were not _____,
(dull/exciting)	but they didn't want _____ lives.
	"Dad makes his living milking
(cows/bulls)	_____. We would prefer riding
(cows/bulls)	_____. His life is _____. We
(dull/exciting)	want ours to be less boring."

READING SKILLS

Guessing Meanings from Context

Choose the best meaning for each italicized word. Use the context to help you.

1. The noisy crowd suddenly becomes quiet; the gray, wooden gate *swings* open; and we see our first cowboy.
   a. moves along rhythmically
   b. hits something with your arm
   c. moves forward or backward

2. He stays on the animal's back just seven seconds before it *bucks* him off, and he lands on the ground of the dusty arena.
   a. slang for dollars
   b. male goats
   c. throws

3. Cattle *wrestlers* try to throw an animal to the ground.
   a. people who try hard to do something
   b. people who try to throw down a human or an animal
   c. people who work with cattle

4. He gets up, *dusts off* his jeans, and runs out of the arena.
   a. puts dust on something
   b. removes dust from something
   c. prepares to use again

5. The longer the cowboy stays on, the more *prize* money he wins.
   a. something given for winning a contest
   b. outstanding
   c. something very expensive

Connections

Connect the underlined word or groups of words to the idea they refer to. Look at the example on page 85 if necessary.

We see our first cowboy. He is riding a wild, bucking 1500-pound bull. <u>He</u> stays on the <u>animal's</u> back for just seven seconds before <u>it</u> bucks him off, and he lands on the ground of the dusty arena. For a moment, the cowboy lies <u>there,</u> and the angry bull moves toward <u>him.</u> A rodeo clown runs up to the animal and waves a large, red handkerchief. He uses <u>it</u> to get the animal's attention. The bull notices the colorfully dressed <u>man</u> and starts toward <u>him.</u>

Main Ideas Choose the main idea. The main idea of

1. paragraph 1 is:
   a. The rodeo begins with a bull-riding event.
   b. A colorful clown waves a red handkerchief to attract the bull's attention.
   c. It is time for another cowboy to enter the arena.

2. paragraph 3 is:
   a. Calf roping is the main rodeo event.
   b. Rodeo clowns make crowds laugh and save lives.
   c. Besides bull riding, there are several other typical rodeo events.

3. paragraph 5 is:
   a. The top cowboys usually have planes.
   b. Paul Tierney has to work hard.
   c. Cowboys don't have easy lives.

4. paragraph 6 is:
   a. Competing in rodeos is dangerous.
   b. Don Gay has never been seriously injured.
   c. Don Gay once had 63 stitches.

5. paragraph 7 is:
   a. Cowboys take part in rodeos for different reasons.
   b. Mike Waters does not want a dull, ordinary life.
   c. Rodeos are no big deal for cowboys.

READING 2 Read the passage carefully to learn the answer to this question:

Where do people learn to be cowboys or cowgirls?

Little Dreamers

Lots of little boys and girls all over the world have a dream. They 1
want to be cowboys or cowgirls when they grow up. Today, more and
more of these children see their dream come true. They grow up to
be rodeo cowboys and cowgirls. The rodeo business is good all over
North America, and so is the business of training future rodeo com- 5
petitors. In fact, there are more than a dozen top rodeo schools for
this purpose. Trainees come from all over the United States and
Canada, not just the southwest part of North America.

Bud Sankey and his two sons, Lyle and Ike, run one of the top
rodeo-training schools in the United States. The students in one train-   10
ing session were from ages 7 to 32. Some were beginners, others
almost professional. Many of Sankey's students are from cities, not
from ranches as they were in the owner's childhood. Most of Sankey's
students want to learn bull riding. One of these people is a 30-year-old
bachelor from Wyoming. He plans to ride until he finds a wife.   15
Another was only 10 years old. He started riding bulls when he was 8.

The youngest cowboy at the Sankey school was a 7-year-old boy.
His mother took pictures of him as the instructors put him on a small
calf instead of a bull. The boy fell off and screamed for his mother.
"It's O.K.," she said. "Mommy will rub it where it hurts and make   20
it all better."

Many of the champion cowboys today also started similar training
at the age of 7 or 8. Some of these children belonged to Little Britches, a rodeo organization started in 1952. Little Britches holds local
rodeos with events such as barrel racing and calf riding.   25

Many of the children in Little Britches later compete in college
rodeos. These are similar to the professional rodeos, but without the
prize money. Instead, these college cowboys and cowgirls from one
school compete against those from another. More than 3000 college
students compete in over 100 intercollegiate rodeos each year. After   30
they graduate, some of these young people become professional cowboys and cowgirls. A few of them go on to become rodeo champions.

**COMPREHENSION
CHECK**

Answer these questions:

1. How is the rodeo business in North America?
2. Where do trainees come from?
3. Who is Bud Sankey?
4. What do most of Sankey's students want to learn?
5. How old was the youngest cowboy at the Sankey school?
6. What is Little Britches?
7. What are intercollegiate rodeos? How do they differ from professional rodeos?

VOCABULARY SKILLS

Word Families

training (noun)	He received on-the-job *training*. New employees receive job *training* information.
trainer (noun-person)	*Trainers* help *trainees* learn new skills.
trainee (noun-person)	

train (verb)
  trained
  training
	She *trains* animals.

Fill in the blanks with the appropriate forms:

Athletes _____ regularly to stay in good condition.

They often work with _____ who supervise athletic

_____. The _____ usually are on special diets and

exercise programs. Their _____ usually help plan these.

Affixes   The prefix *inter-* often means "between," "among," or "with."

Examples

1. Mike Waters, a former *International* Rodeo Association World Champion Cowboy, says he does not want to live a dull, ordinary life.   =   Waters, former champion cowboy of an organization *with members from more than one nation*, does not want a dull life.

2. More than 3000 college students compete in over 100 *intercollegiate* rodeos each year.   =   These students take part in over 100 rodeo competitions *between colleges*.

Read the following sentences. Use the context to help you decide the meaning of the italicized words. Then write the meaning in the space provided.

1. There are *intercultural* activities at most colleges to help students learn about different cultures.

_____

2. The head of the organization wanted to meet with members from every department, so she called an *interdepartmental* meeting.

_____

3. Some people do not approve of *interracial* marriages. They fear racially mixed couples will face problems.

_____

4. An *interview* gives both an employer and the future employee a chance to talk to one another and learn each other's views or ideas.

_____

5. We used an *intercom* to talk to each other between rooms.

_____

6. We used an *interstate* highway to get from New York to New Jersey.

_____

READING SKILLS

Guessing Meanings from Context

Choose the best meaning for each italicized word. Use the context to help you.

1. Bud Sankey and his two sons, Lyle and Ike, *run* one of the top rodeo training schools in the United States.
   a. race
   b. manage
   c. train

2. Many of Sankey's students are from cities, not from *ranches* as they were in the owner's childhood.
   a. a large country house where cowboys live
   b. a large land area where animals are raised
   c. a place where vegetables are grown

3. One of these people is a 30-year-old *bachelor* from Wyoming. He plans to ride until he finds a wife.
   a. an unmarried man
   b. a middle-aged man
   c. a beginning bull rider

Connections   Connect the underlined word or words to the idea they refer to. Look at the example on page 85 if necessary.

1. Lots of little boys and girls all over the world have a dream. They want to be cowboys and cowgirls when they grow up. Today, more and more of <u>these children</u> see <u>their dream</u> come true.

2. The rodeo business is good all over North America, and so is the business of training future rodeo competitors. In fact, there are more than a dozen top rodeo schools for <u>this purpose.</u>

3. The students in one training session were from ages 7 to 32. <u>Some</u> were beginners, <u>others</u> almost professional.

4. Many of Sankey's students are from cities, not from ranches as <u>they</u> were in the <u>owner's</u> childhood.

5. Most of Sankey's students want to learn bull riding. <u>One of these people</u> is a 30-year-old bachelor from Wyoming. <u>Another</u> is only 10 years old.

Sentence Splitting   Many sentences are made from more than one sentence. Look at these examples:

> Henry Fonda, who was a famous actor, first began acting in the Omaha Community Playhouse in 1925.

The sentence contains two sentences:

1. Henry Fonda first began acting in the Omaha Community Playhouse in 1925.
2. Henry Fonda was a famous actor.

> Sister Madonna Bruder, who was the first nun to run in the Boston Marathon, finished in 3 hours and 22 minutes.

The sentence contains these two sentences:

1. Sister Madonna Bruder finished in 3 hours and 22 minutes.
2. Sister Madonna Bruder was the first nun to run in the Boston Marathon.

Split the following sentences. You may need to delete certain words.

A. One of these people is a 30-year-old bachelor who plans to ride until he finds a wife.

   1. _____

   2. _____

B. Many of the children in Little Britches later compete in college rodeos which are similar to the professional rodeos.

   1. _____

   2. _____

C. Cowboys who want to make as much money as Paul Tierney have to work hard.

   1. _____

   2. _____

D. Mike Waters, who is a former International Rodeo Association World Champion Cowboy, says he does not want to live a dull, ordinary life.

   1. _____

   2. _____

E. Some of these children belonged to Little Britches, which is a rodeo organization started in 1952.

   1. _____

   2. _____

CHAPTER REVIEW

1. List some of the events at a rodeo:

_____

_____

_____

_____

2. List two reasons why cowboys like their work:

_____

_____

3. Tell about Bud Sankey:

_____

_____

_____

**POST-READING
ACTIVITY**

All the words for this puzzle are connected with the themes from the 18 chapters in this book. The words are in alphabetical order and are grouped by the number of letters in each word. Put the words into the correct places in the puzzle.

3 letters
act
ask (questions)
fun

4 letters
arts (and crafts)
boys
corn
easy (reading)
kids (at camp)
lose (weight)

5 letters
adult (education)
camps
clams
picks (strawberries)
rodeo
sport
straw (hats)
Texas
theme (of chapters)

6 letters
babies
houses
nomads
old man
weight

7 letters
cartoon
cowboys
running
theater

8 letters
balloons
clambake
festival
Labor Day
marathon
trailers

9 letters
computers
education
McDonald's

10 letters
basketball
hamburgers
strawberry
Walt Disney

11 letters
garage sales
Mickey Mouse
underground (houses)

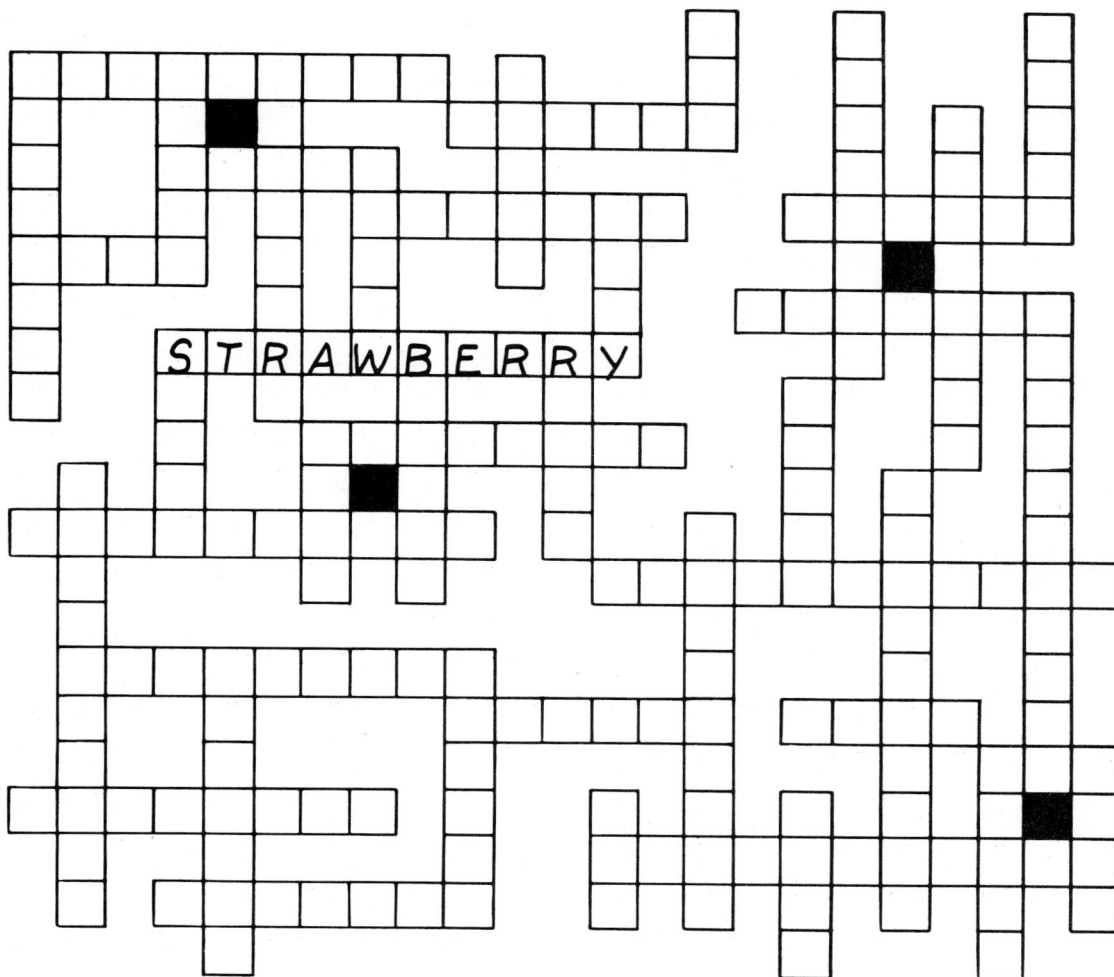

Sources Consulted

Chapter 2   "Computer Camps for Kids." *Newsweek,* July 19, 1982.

Pierce, K. M. and C. Crooks. "Camps for Computers." *Time,* August 3, 1981

Chapter 3   Rickman, R. "Strawberry Time." *Des Moines Sunday Register Picture Magazine,* June 7, 1981.

Chapter 4   Hill, D. R. and R. Abramson. "West Indian Carnival in Brooklyn." *Natural History,* August/September 1979.

Chapter 5   Gault, C. and F. Gault. *The Harlem Globetrotters and Basketball's Funniest Games.* New York: Walker and Co., 1977.

Chapter 6   Fracchia, C. *Converted into Houses.* New York: Viking Press, 1976.

Martindale, D. "New Homes Revive the Ancient Art of Living Underground." *Smithsonian,* February 1979.

Thompson, L. K. "Below Ground Living." *Workbench,* March 1979.

"Weekend in a Corn Crib." *House and Garden,* August 1979.

Chapter 7   Herzig, A. C. and J. L. Mali. *Oh, Boy! Babies!* Boston: Little, Brown and Co., 1980.

Chapter 8   Brewster, T. A. "Mickey Mouse at Fifty: Celebrating with a Collector." *Americana,* November/December 1978.

Thomas, B. *Walt Disney: An American Original.* New York: Simon & Schuster, 1976.

Chapter 9   Baker, J. F. "PW Interviews Bob Waligunda." *Publishers Weekly,* October 9, 1981.

Hall, S. M. and N. Harrison. "The 'Eagle' Has Disbanded: America's Top Balloonists Race Each Other—and Fate." *People,* February 16, 1981.

Hayes, W. *The Complete Ballooning Book.* Mountain View, Ca.: World Publications, 1977.

Morgan, L. "Plucky Pierre: Getting High in the 1700's." *Flying,* May 1979.

Yost, E. "The Longest Manned Balloon Flight." *National Geographic,* February 1977.

Chapter 10   "The Houses that Love Builds." *Reader's Digest,* June 1981.

Kottack, C. P. "Rituals at McDonald's." *Natural History,* January 1978.

Kroc, R. *Grinding It Out: The Making of McDonald's.* Chicago: H. Regnery, 1977.

Kroc, R. and R. Anderson. "Grinding It Out." *Saturday Evening Post,* March 1978.

"Still the Champion." *Time,* April 25, 1977.

Will, G. F. "The Art of Hamburger." *Newsweek,* February 20, 1978.

Chapter 11   "Education: Home Study Courses Come of Age." *Glamour,* February 1983.

"Federal Study on Home-Study Courses." *U.S. News and World Report,* July 9, 1979.

"For Adults: The Pleasures and Profits of Learning." *Changing Times,* December 1980.

"Grownups at School: A Class for Every Taste and Time." *Vogue,* August 1979.

"Live and Learn." *50 Plus,* October 1980.

Chapter 12   "As 70 Million Americans Try to Shed Weight—." *U.S. News and World Report,* December 22, 1980.

"California Health Spas: Reducing Weight, Worries and Wallets." *Travel/Holiday,* October 1980.

"Weight Watchers: Think Thin and Grow Fat." *Nation's Business,* September 1978.

Chapter 14   Bridges, B. *Great American Chili Book.* New York: Rawson, Wade, 1981.

Fossel, P. "A Summer Feast." *Americana,* July 1979.

Neely, M. and W. Neely. *International Chili Society Official Chili Cookbook.* New York: St. Martin's, 1981.

Sokolov, R. "An Original Old-Fashioned Yankee Clambake." *Natural History,* June 1980.

Chapter 15 Callahan, T. "The Joy Is Running Out." *Newsweek,* April 19, 1982.

Cimons, M. "How Women Got to Run the Distance." *MS.,* July 1981.

Lance, K. *Running for Health and Beauty.* Indianapolis: Bobbs-Merrill Co., 1977.

Martin, D. and Gynn, R. *The Marathon Footrace.* Springfield, Ill.: Charles C Thomas, 1979.

Shatenstein, E. "Women's Running." *Runner's World,* July 1982.

"Runner's World Up-Date." *Runner's World,* July 1982.

Will, G. "Run for Your Life." *Newsweek,* April 19, 1976.

"Women on the Run." *Newsweek,* November 14, 1977.

Chapter 16 Trillin, C. "U.S. Journal On the Road: Wally Byam Caravan for Automobile Trailers." *New Yorker,* October 16, 1978.

Chapter 17 Dean, A. *Little Theater Organization and Management.* New York:

Appleton and Co., 1926.

Nadel, N. "The Sunday Actor." *Horizon,* March 1980.

"Start a Community Theater." *Mother Earth News,* April 1980.

Chapter 18 Demaret, K. "Jocks; Women Rodeo Champions J. Haynes and S. Pirtle." *People,* May 1, 1978.

Eyman, S. "Rodeo Is Riding High Again." *New York Times Magazine,* September 20, 1981.

Martin, F. W. "Rodeo Star Don Gay Has Learned to Grab the Bull by the Horns Before It Grabs Him." *People,* July 27, 1981.

O'Neil, P. "Folk Heroics of Rodeo Have Become Organized, Mechanized— and Profitable." *Smithsonian,* March 1979.

Word Games Answer Key

page 12

1. AND
2. PAN
3. HAND
4. PLANT

5. WANT
6. CLEAN
7. ANSWER
8. MANY

page 13

	¹D	R	E	S	S		
²S	H	O	E	S			
	³T	O	A	S	T	E	R
		⁴D	R	A	W	E	R
	⁵S	U	I	T			
⁶P	L	A	N	T			
	⁷R	U	G				

page 28

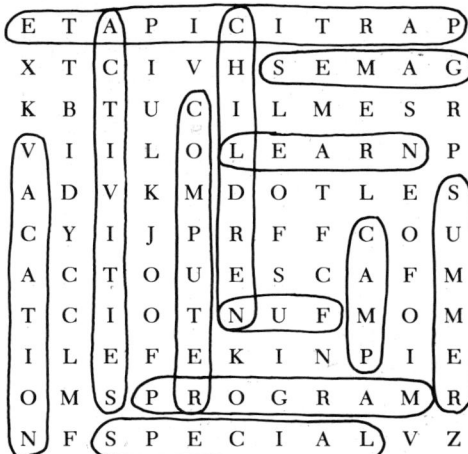

```
E T A P I C I T R A P
X T C I V H S E M A G
K B T U C I L M E S R
V I I L O L E A R N P
A D V K M D O T L E S
C Y I J P R F F C O U
A C T O U E S C A F M
T I O T N U F M O M M
I L E F E K I N P I E
O M S P R O G R A M R
N F S P E C I A L V Z
```

page 42

1. SING
2. FIND
3. THING
4. RIDING
5. DINNER

6. MAGAZINE
7. MINUTE
8. WINTER
9. FINISH

page 43

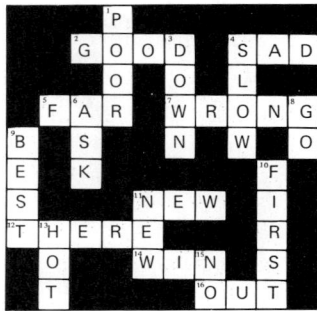

page 58

see	hear	top
eat	are	open
at	ear	pen
the	rest	pens
he	stop	opens

page 59

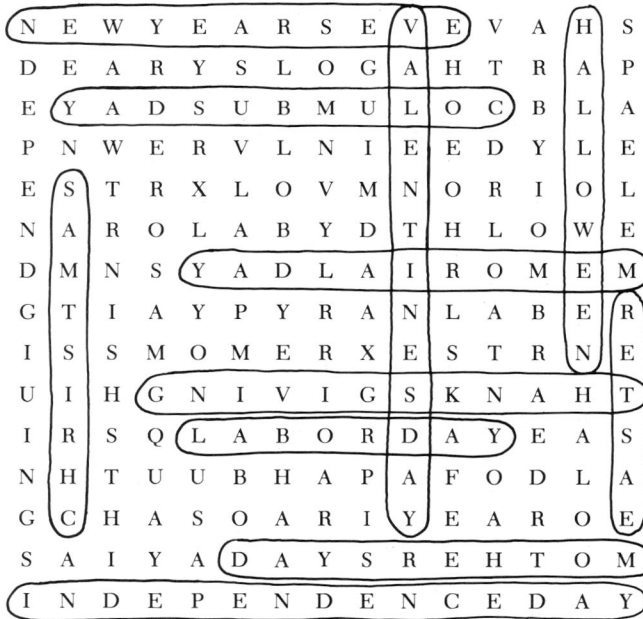

page 71

1. MONEY   5. VACATION
2. ONCE   6. STRONG
3. NOON   7. SECOND
4. SPOON   8. SEASON

page 72

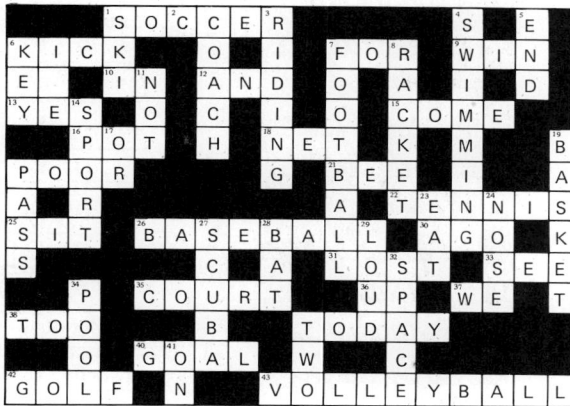

page 89

1. FOR
2. WORK
3. CORN
4. DOOR
5. SPORT
6. STORE
7. HORSE
8. FLOOR
9. UNIFORM
10. NEIGHBOR

page 105

1. LITTLE
2. SKIING
3. SOCCER
4. DOLLAR
5. BUTTER
6. PASSES
7. WINNER
8. LETTER
9. TENNIS
10. SUMMER
11. SITTER
12. SCANNING

page 120

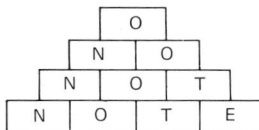

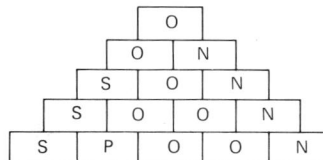

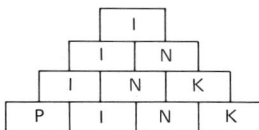

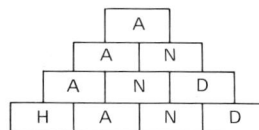

page 135

Maxie *Anderson*

Denison *Bollay*

John *Bonard*

Walt *Disney*

Bob *Furleigh*

Ub *Iwerks*

Charles *Lindbergh*

Mickey *Mouse*

Eleanor *Roosevelt*

Abe *Saperstein*

Bill *Woodman*

```
A  H  G  I  E  L  R  U  F  N
B  O  L  L  A  Y  A  X  I  E
E  R  O  O  S  E  V  E  L  T
C  O  R  K  E  N  T  U  B  E
A  N  D  E  R  S  O  N  Y  S
P  E  A  O  R  I  S  O  N  U
H  G  R  E  B  D  N  I  L  O
A  R  P  D  R  A  N  O  B  M
N  A  M  D  O  O  W  A  L  T
S  K  R  E  W  I  C  K  E  Y
```

page 155

```
D  R  I  N  K  S  E  C  I  G  C  E  T  F  C  B  T  R
T  A  F  H  N  S  L  E  T  T  U  C  E  I  N  I  E  N
A  D  E  R  E  G  R  U  B  M  A  H  H  I  A  G  D  C
N  L  R  S  U  H  A  N  U  M  U  I  T  A  R  M  E  S
M  I  E  K  S  I  A  S  E  S  Q  C  O  U  A  A  E  E
I  L  D  A  K  S  T  A  R  D  U  K  B  Y  O  C  S  I
L  P  N  H  N  A  A  P  I  E  A  E  O  R  P  W  E  R
K  I  U  E  R  C  S  T  I  M  S  N  Q  U  X  A  M  F
S  C  O  D  N  O  I  N  O  E  N  M  H  A  T  B  A  H
H  L  P  O  N  O  N  Y  E  A  S  C  O  O  R  A  S  C
A  K  R  U  A  K  E  H  I  P  T  N  E  N  A  M  E  N
K  E  B  I  I  C  S  R  E  S  U  N  D  A  E  S  S  E
E  C  T  L  S  E  E  C  K  A  R  G  O  R  I  N  K  R
S  H  R  D  L  S  T  I  R  D  Y  G  N  I  N  O  S  F
O  E  A  B  O  N  A  F  I  L  L  E  T  O  F  I  S  H
U  E  U  R  C  B  N  I  C  F  H  T  S  N  O  I  N  O
N  O  Q  U  A  P  I  C  K  L  E  S  H  K  E  S  H  I
D  R  I  N  R  T  R  E  G  R  U  B  E  S  E  E  H  C
```

page 171

1. ITEMS
2. KITCHEN
3. WITH
4. SUIT
5. WRITE
6. WAIT
7. FRUIT

page 186

artificial/real
expensive—cheap
first—last
forget—remember
important—unimportant
keep—throw away
learn—teach
loudly—softly
thin—fat

receive/give
new—used
private—public
sell—buy
useful—useless
usual—unusual
young—old
easy—hard
lose—gain

page 187

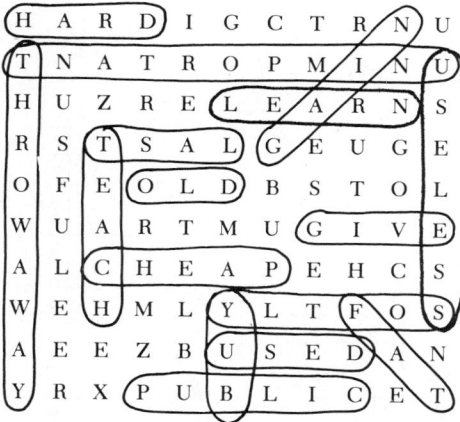

page 201

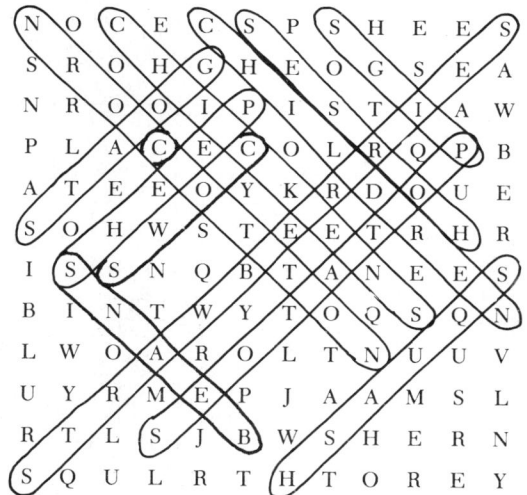

page 215

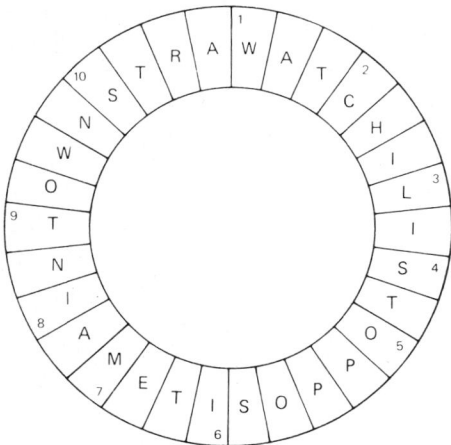

page 229

Here are twenty-five words. You may have more.

are	head
art	read
die	ride
her	tire
not	redo
one	ears
red	heard
sad	heart
done	stone
east	tired
hear	tried
here	hears
hard	

page 245

The people from Florida have the monkey.

	RED	YELLOW	GREEN	BLUE	ORANGE
STATE	CALIFORNIA	FLORIDA	VIRGINIA	SOUTH DAKOTA	OREGON
DESTINATION	WASHINGTON	DALLAS	ROCKY MTS.	DISNEYLAND	NEW ORLEANS
VEHICLE	TRUCK	MERCEDES	VAN	STATION WGN.	LAND ROVER
PET	PARROT	MONKEY	POODLE	CAT	SNAKE

page 259

page 275

93 94 95 96 20 19 18 17 16 15 14 13 12